Dedicated to

My Daughter, Marisa

and

My Son, William

Other books published by Clari Diaz

Cooking and Telling Stories y El Pilon
It's All About Family

TABLE OF CONTENTS

INTRODUCTION

When my daughter, Marisa, reached 19 years of age, I decided it was time to put pen to paper and document her story. She has known she was adopted from the tender age of five, when, like most young children, she asked, "Mommy did I come out of your belly?" I certainly didn't expect that particular question on that particular day. She already knew that mommy went to Paraguay to have her join our family. But she didn't quite understand yet what that meant. I knew that of course. As the parent of an adopted child, I wanted to create an early foundation for her.

Marisa was a bright little girl. I intuitively recognized that the question "Where do I come from?" was going to come early. I read many books about raising adopted children, so I would know how to handle the question. I learned that when adopted children ask a question about their birth, it's best to simply answer the question and wait to see if other questions come through their young innocent mind. Of course, when the question did come, I was surprised, but I felt relieved that I knew how to answer it. So, when Marisa asked the question at five years of age, I took a deep breath and said, "No." The look on her face broke my heart into tiny little pieces. Those pieces could not compare to the shock on her little face. I immediately felt a deep pain in my heart that went to the pit of my stomach. I knew from her reaction, she didn't expect me to say "No." Oh God, I dreaded this moment and here it was! All I wanted to do was protect her, hold her, and calm her fears.

She was a very smart little girl. So, the next obvious question followed. "Whose belly did I come out of mommy?" I saw confusion in her beautiful, little face. Oh God, I thought, help me here. And suddenly the words came to me, "Remember when I told you I went to Paraguay to pick you up and bring you home?" She said, "Yes." "Well, a very special woman from Paraguay carried you in her belly and made a very big sacrifice to give you to me. She said, "Oh." Then she looked at me and said, "Mommy, can I have pancakes please for breakfast?" I said, "Of course, but only if you help me make them." She took my hand and we both walked to the kitchen. I slowly began to breathe a little easier with my little girl's hand in mine and I made a mental note to never forget this first dialogue between my young daughter and me about her birth.

I felt devastated inside by her question, and shocked that it came so soon, and relieved that I still had a reprieve. Of course, she didn't really understand what those words meant. I was afraid of how being adopted was going to manifest within her, once she did comprehend.

My instinct as a mother was to protect her always. I went over in my mind a thousand times the notion of not ever telling her that she was adopted. But, I knew I couldn't do that. I would hurt her more by not telling her the truth.

Because I had read several books about adoption, I knew not to elaborate; just answer the questions when young children first ask about their birth. Marisa loved her story and she asked me to tell her the story about when I went to Paraguay over and over again. I had a photo album that went along with the story, which she loved so much. I knew that one day I would write this book about our special journey, to help her understand how much she is loved and cherished.

What I didn't expect was that, upon adopting a second child, this scenario would repeat itself once again, and I was not prepared like I was for Marisa. When my young, adopted son William, also at the tender age of five, asked if he came out of my belly, I was in shock. I asked him if he had spoken to his sister about this. Marisa was then ten years old. But he said, "No." So, I answered him the very same way I answered Marisa and he also asked, "Whose belly did I come out of?" He was in shock. Seeing the exact same expression on his little face that his sister had was truly overwhelming. I don't know why I thought he would never ask. After all, there were no pictures of me with a big belly anywhere. He didn't ask for breakfast. Instead, he wanted to know if his real parents were dead. Oh God, I was not prepared for that. He was so inquisitive. So, I said, "I don't really know," which was the truth. Then he said to me, "I'm so glad you're my mommy." I said, "Me too." And that was it.

In 2006, I started writing my memoir. And like a great book that you can't put down to even eat or drink anything, my mind melded with the computer capturing every thought, like Spock on Star Trek when he did his mind-meld, "My thoughts are your thoughts.... We are one." Well, in the same manner as Spock, I was one with the computer. I wrote for one week straight, with one day lasting for more than 12 hours with no lunch or dinner. When I finally came back to the present, I wondered if this was how writers get when they feel the need to put all their thoughts on paper before they're lost. I felt consumed by my own story and once I started writing, I simply couldn't stop, and only did out of absolute shear exhaustion.

Writing this story created a new sense of immeasurable joy, re-living this very special time in my life. Looking back nearly 30 years, I discovered that my thoughts, my prayers, and my wishes led me through this amazing journey with all the various crossroads that provided challenges, and at the same time, discovery about myself through moments of despair, sadness, joy and motherhood. My faith in God helped me when I felt hopeless. During the tough times in my life, I had several conversations with God that were very insightful. I learned that what you sincerely desire, you attract. And, the crossroads that developed were incredible in so many ways, finally culminating in motherhood. But, when you start a journey, you must begin at the beginning.

Chapter 1:

First Steps

1980

I couldn't believe I had my period yet again this month. I was not taking birth control and I was not being too careful practicing the "rhythm method." I should have been pregnant. I knew something was wrong. As we were getting dressed to go to work one morning, I announced to my husband, "Honey, next week we are going to make love for five days straight! What do you think?" "I am ready whenever you are, sweetheart!"

I giggled at his response. He gave me a great big hug and held me close. And then he said to me, "Are you worried about something?" I answered softly and shyly. "Well, I should be pregnant. You know that we haven't been too careful lately." He looked at me confused and asked, "Why are you worried? We have only been married for a little over two years. I thought we were going to wait until our fifth year." I said, "Yes, I know but, I just got my period and you know I think I should have been pregnant. I think there is something wrong with me. You know my mom never conceived after giving birth to Sonia. So, this could be hereditary."

Then my husband responded, "You know this little experiment could just get you pregnant. Are you sure you want to do this? I for one am not ready to start a family. We agreed," he reminded me. I responded, "But if there is a problem, then I need to find out now." He counseled me, "Why don't you just see your GYN physician first? Not that I mind being your guinea pig." We both started laughing. He had great sense of humor and always made me laugh. Then he said, "You work right in the hospital. Make the appointment and get yourself checked out." Of course, why didn't I think of that! He was so right.

At that time, I worked as an Administrative Assistant for Montefiore Medical Center in the Bronx. So, that morning, I made an appointment to see my GYN physician, Dr. Suarez. She was a young, Hispanic Gynecologist, which was a rarity back in the 1980s. I had been seeing her for a year and I liked her a great deal. Working in a huge hospital had its perks. Two weeks later, there I was on my lunch hour talking to Dr. Suarez about my fears that I might have a problem conceiving a baby. I felt very comfortable speaking to her about my fears, which were so personal.

"Clari, I can understand your concerns, especially since you are not really using birth control." However, before I submit you to a series of tests, have your husband come to my office and submit a sperm sample. Have him call first, before he arrives, so I can alert my staff. We have to rule him out first, then we can concentrate on you a little more in-depth. I am just going to do a general check-up, do a pap smear and take some blood for now. Do you have any other questions?" No, I really didn't.

I came home that night, with "the cup." Actually, it was a cup to collect a urine sample, but I wanted to tease my husband a little to take the edge off. When he went to take a bath, I snuck in the shower. "Hi, like some company?" He was smiling. Then I filled him in on my appointment with Dr. Suarez.

"Darling, I hate to tell you, but you need to submit a sperm sample." He made a face. Then I said, "I could help. You need to fill this cup." "Oh shit!" Then he said laughing, "Well I just might need that help you are offering." I giggled. We bathed each other and then I told him he had to actually go to the doctor's office to submit his "specimen." He made a face again. I knew this was embarrassing for him. Heck, I was embarrassed telling him he had to do this. I tried to make the whole thing a little humorous to silence my fears and brush away the thoughts that were starting to nag my mind. I gave my husband Dr. Suarez' business card and he promised to make an appointment that week.

Chapter 2:

Intuition

I always thought I had a sixth sense about things, not realizing that I actually had a great gift of intuition. Unfortunately, there were no books like *The Secret* back then to help me sort out my thoughts. But, in the end, I convinced myself that I really did have a gift. My intuition was very strong and it scared me at times. I didn't know how to channel the thoughts that came to me and sometimes, I felt that it affected the people around me. But, I recognized that life is a learning process and as you grow in years and in faith, you discover your special gifts.

The first time my intuition manifested itself, I was approaching sixteen years of age. I was living in the projects in the Bronx with my parents. My parents were born in Puerto Rico and they relocated to New York City in the early 1950's, as soon as they married. Actually, my dad sent my mom to live with his parents, who were already living in New York, just three days after their wedding day. Dad followed six months later, after he accumulated additional income. We had been living in the projects for about eleven years and the neighborhood was slowly changing for the worse. I was their only child. I had a sister named Sonia, but she died at the age of two from pneumonia when I was six years old. My mom was never able to conceive again. The projects where we lived were initially only for working families, but slowly, the projects were taking families on "Section Eight" and the neighborhood was slowly changing for the worse. Many working families were moving out and I know my parents wanted to move out as well.

In October of 1969, there was a series of apartment robberies in the neighborhood and I had this awful feeling that we were going to be next. A month before my sixteenth birthday, I told my dad we should get an alarm installed for our front door. My birthday was fast approaching on November 19th. My parents were planning a big sweet sixteen birthday party for me at our home. I was really excited about it, but I also had this strange feeling that there was not going to be a party. I didn't send out formal invitations about my party. My parents told me that I could invite a few of my close friends. One of my best friends told me that some kids from the neighborhood were going to crash my party. I suddenly became nervous about this, in addition to the robberies in the neighborhood. None of the robberies were in our building, but just the same, I had this terrible feeling that we were going to be robbed. The more my birthday drew closer, the more I didn't want the party. I decided to tell my dad about my feelings about the robberies. He told me that he was worried, too. Well, several days before my birthday, my dad called The ABC Alarm Company that was advertising on the Spanish channel, Channel 47. They were supposed to come to our home Monday night, November 17. But they didn't show up. My dad called again. The company promised to send a technician the very next day. But on Tuesday, November 18, no one came to our home. My dad decided to call another company that promised to come on the weekend. When no one came from the ABC Alarm Company, I knew we were going to get robbed. The intuition I felt was that strong. Well, my awful premonition came true. The very next day on Wednesday, November 19th, on my sixteenth birthday, we got robbed.

When my parents and I arrived at our apartment, the cylinder was gone from our front door. A gaping hole revealed where the cylinder used to be. My father held me back from entering and, as he slowly opened the door, I could see that our apartment had been ransacked in the worst way. My father asked me and my mother not to come in until he was sure no one was in the apartment. I knew that our neighbors had to know what happened, but nobody was saying anything. I finally came in and ran to my room. The little bit of jewelry I had was gone. The few precious leather bags I possessed were gone. All my draws were open, and my clothing was scattered all over the floor. I just sat on the floor surrounded by my clothes and cried my eyes out. My parents canceled my sweet sixteen party. Our apartment was such a mess. What hurt me most was seeing both my parents crying that night. There are moments in your life that you never forget and seeing my parents holding onto each other crying in our ransacked apartment will stay in my memory forever. We felt so violated. That night my father sat in the living room with a machete in his hand. He didn't sleep all night watching over us and the little we had left.

Did I attract this awful thing to happen to us? The mind is so powerful. I knew I didn't want that party and I was afraid that we would get robbed. I remember how strong the premonitions were back then. They scared me. But when we were robbed, I really got scared. Over the years, however, I learned to trust my intuition. It truly was a gift.

1975

It was the summer of 1975, when my special gift manifested itself once again. That year, I got engaged to Jorge at the age of 22. He was my high school sweetheart. We met when I was a senior in high school and he was junior. I was one year older than him. We got engaged when we were in the fourth year of our relationship. I was in my second year of college and Jorge was in his first year of college at John Jay. That's when I started having a recurring dream. I saw myself walking down the aisle in a white wedding dress. I could see Jorge standing by the alter, but his back was to me. When I finally got to him, he slowly turned around and I looked up and saw the person I thought was my fiancé had no face! I would then wake up startled. I sadly realized, after having this dream several times, that I was not going to marry him. In reality, I knew I didn't want to marry him. I could sense that he was not the man who was supposed to be my husband. But, I was scared because I did have deep feelings for him.

During this time, I was working as a part-time secretary at Question Education Products, a large toy manufacturing company in the Bronx. Jorge was going to John Jay College. I was living in Coop City in the Bronx with my parents. We had moved there in August of 1974. The Coop was beautiful, and I was so happy to finally get out of the projects. We were only living in Coop City for eight months when, in April of 1975, I met a couple of young Hispanic people in the neighborhood and joined the Spanish American Community Club (SACC). It was a place to meet new Hispanic families of our same culture, find out about the community, and attend community events. The club was just starting a Single's Club. Yolanda, who lived in my building, and I became friends and we went together to one of the meetings to find out more about the Single's Club. The Vice President of SACC was young guy named Edwin. He was starting the Single's Club and he impressed me a great deal. I was attracted to the way he spoke with confidence and charm. He had this beard which really made him look sexy. He was taking names for the Single's Club, so Yolanda and I both joined immediately. I admit it, we were being bad. Well, maybe not her, but I was. I wanted to know more about him.

Edwin and I got to know each other as I attended the Single's Club meetings and participated in some of the functions in May and June. One day in late June, he asked me to go out with him and I didn't know what to say because I wasn't free to date him. I felt so bad because I was flirting, and I was being deceitful. So, I told him the truth that I was engaged and naturally he was very surprised and hurt since I never said anything about my situation before. In truth, I was very confused about my relationship with

Jorge. He rarely came to see me, and we weren't going out much anymore.

I decided to tell Jorge about my feelings for Edwin and as a result I thought we should give each other some space. I thought he would easily agree. He only came to see me on Sundays and then he would leave until the following week or two. Well, at first, he was shocked when I told him how I felt. He convinced me that things would change between us and I believed him. So, Jorge started to take me out on Saturdays and I decided to continue with the engagement, I still loved him a great deal. Jorge asked me to leave the club, which I did. But Edwin would call me from time to time. I would sometimes bump into him in the neighborhood. We would walk around and talk about things, sometimes about my engagement. Edwin knew I wasn't happy. Several times he sent me "Thinking of You" cards and one day he sent me a five-page letter where he intelligently presented the pros and cons about dating him and also expressed his strong feelings. I was so confused. Edwin was so smart, and he had just graduated from Fordham University in May and was going to graduate school for his master's degree in Bilingual Education. He wanted to be a teacher. His future was set, and I was drawn to him by his ambition, confidence and good looks. Plus, he was genuinely a nice guy. I went to my father about my feelings. He cautioned to guard my heart and not be deceitful or impulsive and that only I could get hurt if I did the wrong thing. "Put it in God's hands," he counseled me.

So, one evening, before I went to bed, I had a conversation with God. I was still for a long time and almost felt like someone was holding me close. I prayed softly and whispered, "Dear God I am so confused. Dad says I shouldn't date Edwin on the sly because I am playing with fire and in the end, I will end up getting burned....... You know what I mean. But I don't think Jorge loves me. Please show me a sign. I don't know what to do and I don't want to do the wrong thing. Your will is always my command. Amen." I made the sign of the cross and went to sleep feeling at peace. That very evening, I had a dream.

I dreamt that I was swimming in a huge pool. Around the pool were people talking and drinking. I realized I was at a pool party, but I was the only one in the pool. I started swimming around and when I came up, I saw Jorge talking to a woman. She was pregnant. "Who is this girl," I asked myself in the dream? I started to swim again and then I spotted my girlfriend, Nancy. She started to walk towards Jorge and the pregnant girl and then I saw them all talking together. Then I woke up thinking...that was weird, especially since I hadn't seen Nancy in a long time. Maybe she is pregnant. We went to the same college together, but she graduated a year ahead of me with a nursing degree.

The next day was Sunday and I was having breakfast when suddenly our doorbell rang. I went to see who it was, and it was Nancy, my girlfriend! As I opened the door, I found myself saying, "Nancy, what a surprise to see you!"

Upon entering, Nancy said, "I was visiting my mother and I decided to stop by to see you." Her mother lived in Coop City. The Coop apartment we now occupied used to belong to Nancy. She was looking to sell it after she graduated from college and move to a house in Long Island with her husband and two girls. She told me about her plans and I asked my parents to go look at the apartment. My mother loved it and my parents decided to buy it. Of course, there was a great deal of persuasion from me. Those were the lucky events that led us to live in Coop City, and then I remembered the dream! "Nancy this is so weird," I said in almost whisper. "I dreamt of you last night." "That is weird," she said. Then I asked her, "Are you pregnant?" She looked at me like I was nuts and said "No, why are asking me that?" Then I said, "It was the dream. How long can you stay? Jorge will be coming over soon and I am sure he would love to see you." She promised to stay until 1:00 p.m. Mom made this fabulous lunch and we chit-chatted about our new jobs and her new house and her two adorable daughters.

Well, one o'clock arrived and went, and no Jorge. Nancy had to leave. I was highly upset. It was already two in the afternoon and Jorge had not called me. Around 2:30 p.m., he finally called and he was crying. He told me something had happened and that he was coming over to speak to me. I immediately told my mother that something was wrong with Jorge. He finally got to my house at 3:00 p.m. and he asked my mom if he could talk to me alone in my bedroom. He was always so polite to mom and always gave her a kiss when he came in. She like him a lot and she told him, "Of course." So off we went to talk in private.

He sat on my bed and I stood over him and waited nervously for him to begin. He looked absolutely awful. His face and nose were red from all the crying. "What happened? You are scaring me," I softly told him. Then he started to speak, "I need to tell you something." It seemed as if he didn't know how to get the words out. He took a deep breath. "I met someone. Her name is Michelle and I grew to cherish her, although I still love you." I didn't know how that was possible, but I kept silent. There was something more to his story. He continued, "My mother followed me to Michelle's house this morning and discovered that she is pregnant. There was a big, awful scene. I wanted you to hear it from me and not from her."

I didn't cry and I wasn't angry. I just asked, "How pregnant is she?" His response really shocked me. "She is nine months." I suddenly remembered the dream and recalled that the woman in the dream appeared very pregnant. God had revealed a sign to me. I then asked him, "How old is she?" This really was a slap in the face. "She is 31 years old." "What!" That, I couldn't comprehend. "She is eleven years older than you Jorge! I thought she was a teenager since you look like death. You must have been involved with her for over a year since she is now nine months pregnant." He didn't say anything, except that he was sorry. I finally said to him, "How selfish can you be? I asked you for some space and you convinced me that you were still interested in our relationship.... that, that you loved me. You could have let me go without causing me this...this awful pain." I was now crying. He had his head down and was crying too. I finally said, "Jorge, I need you to leave." "Clari what do you plan to do? I don't want to lose you." I just said, "Jorge, I need to think, and I have to speak to my parents." He tried to kiss me goodbye, but I wouldn't let him. He left. I sat in my room for a while by myself. My mom came in and found me with tears on my face. I told her what happened. She held me in her arms and I cried some more.

Since it was summer time, my parents took me out on the weekends to keep me from getting depressed. I wasn't really eating and lost so much weight. I was down to a size three and 95 pounds. I was highly upset with myself. I had known something was wrong with Jorge. He was always tired when he came over. He didn't want to go out. But I never suspected what he confessed to me. My parents were upset, as well. They also felt betrayed, so they felt I should end the engagement. I didn't think it was something I could tell him over the phone, since he was honest enough to tell me about Michelle. I called him and asked him to come over to the house. I sat with him and asked how he was. He looked sad and miserable. I put the engagement ring in a box and returned it to him. It was a ring that had been handed down from his grandmother, to his mother, and then, to me. I couldn't keep it. It was a precious heirloom. He then said to me, "I will never give this ring to any other girl." I didn't say anything. He gave me a hug and left. I never saw him again. Just like that he was out of my life forever. That scared me somehow. How can you stop loving someone after close to five years? I felt sadness, relief and freedom all at the same time.

It was September when I received a phone call from Edwin. We talked for two hours and I hadn't told him yet about my situation. He finally opened that door for me. "Clari, when are you going to agree to go out with me? It's obvious that you enjoy speaking with me." In my mind, I was debating whether to tell him or not. The hurt was still so raw. Then, I surprised myself when I blurted out, "Edwin I am not engaged anymore." I told him everything that had transpired during the last month in my life. He heard my voice shake a little, even though I tried to control my emotions. He then asked, "Would your parents mind very much if I came over right now?" "I don't think so." "Well then, I am coming over."

I think he flew because, in five minutes, he was knocking on my door. I opened the door and he took my hand and asked me to take a walk with him. I told my mom. When we got outside, he gave me a great big hug and the sweetest kiss. "Go out with me. I know that you have been hurt, but not all guys are the same." I needed some loving, that was for sure. And my self-esteem was so damn low, too. I felt that I was pretty nice looking, and smart. But that didn't keep Jorge from cheating on me. What made Edwin so different? I was so deeply hurt and scared that history would repeat itself with another guy. So, I told Edwin, "I will agree to go out with you under the conditions that you not expect too much from me. Truthfully, I am a bit apprehensive about going into another relationship. How do I know that you won't hurt me too?" He then said, "Your heart will be like a chalkboard and every day my love for you will slowly erase the hurt." I felt so vulnerable. In truth, I was scared to fall in love again.

But Edwin was so different from Jorge. Six months into our relationship, I felt like I had won the lottery. We went out every Saturday. And on Sundays, we went to church together. And on the ninth of every month, for one entire year, he sent me a card. The ninth was the day in September he came over to my house and asked me to go out with him. In each card, he expressed how he felt and how happy he was with our relationship. Each card read like a diary, indicating what we did together, the places we visited, and the depth of his growing love for me. I started sending him cards too and coincidentally, one day, we sent each other the same card. We laughed a lot about that. The card had a picture of two people standing near their bicycles holding hands. We used to go bike riding a lot around the neighborhood. So, naturally, when we saw the card, we each thought the card was perfect. We really were in-tune with one another.

We got engaged a year later and agreed to set a date when he landed his teaching job. A year into our engagement, he was offered a teaching job in Manhattan and we immediately set a date for the wedding, July 15, 1978. My life was filled with wedding activities and I was a little stressed out since I had also accepted a new job. The salary was great, but the hours were long, and I was going to college at night for my BA in Business Administration.

A few months before the wedding, I had that recurring dream from when I was engaged to Jorge. I was frightened inside my own dream. I wanted to wake up as I was walking down the aisle, but I couldn't wake myself up. I didn't want to see a man with no face. But, when the man at the alter turned around, it was Edwin! I was so damn happy when I woke up! I felt like God was giving me His blessing. I was on the right path. My mother found me dancing all around my room. She thought I was possessed by spirits as she laughingly asked me why I was acting so weird. I hugged her and shouted, "I am getting married!" She replied, "I know that, it's in three months! What is wrong with you?" I said, "Nothing mom, I am just so happy!"

Clari Diaz

Chapter 3:

Infertility

Three years into my marriage with Edwin, I was once again experiencing a terrible premonition. The premonition was as strong as the one I felt when my family got robbed when I was sixteen. I couldn't control my negative thoughts. I felt that something was wrong with Edwin's sperm count. No matter how much I tried to shake this feeling, it wouldn't go away. When the results came back, Dr. Suarez asked to see me. I tried once again to convince myself that it was me. But, I didn't really believe what I was thinking. When I sat in her office, she gave me this serious look, "Clari, this is not good news." My heart was beating so hard I had trouble concentrating on what she was saying. "Your husband has a low sperm count."

Even though I suspected this, hearing those words, the certainty was no less devastating. I felt hopeless and scared. I dared to ask about his sperm count. "How low?" Dr. Suarez then indicted, "Clari, your husband practically has no sperm count." My head shot up with her response. I started to cry right in her office. My thoughts were raging inside. I was saying to myself, "Why him? I was so hoping it was me. I could deal with infertility. I am stronger mentally."

Then she hit me with more bad news when she said, "You also have a problem, but yours can be remedied with medication. Your thyroid count is abnormal. You need to have a CAT scan of the brain, so we can look at your pituitary gland. You should not get pregnant until we get your thyroid level within normal range." Between my tears, I said, "Well Doc, we don't have to worry about that, I can't get pregnant anyway."

At that point, Dr. Suarez got up from behind her desk and came over and put her arms around me and said to me, "I want to give you some good advice. You are only married a little over two years and you are both very young. You have time on your side." She was right. I was only twenty-seven and Edwin was twenty-eight. Then she continued, "Listen to me, your husband might not want to see someone right away. You will need to be very patient and understanding. Men do not handle this type of news well at all. Clari, some marriages don't make it. If you survive this with your husband, I do recommend that he see a male infertility specialist, and you need to see an endocrinologist for your thyroid condition immediately. You will need to be strong."

Five minutes later, I left her office in a daze. I felt like I was carrying a dead body on my back. How was I going to tell Edwin? I started crying again. My heart was so heavy with pain I could barely breathe. I thought of her last comment to me, "Some marriages don't make it!" I made a conscious decision to be strong. Oh God, I was so scared.

I knew for a fact that Edwin was not going to take this well. I took the rest of the afternoon off. I was so damn upset. I didn't know how I was going to tell him. What words do I use to soften the blow? I knew intuitively I couldn't talk to anyone about this. I didn't even think about what this news meant for me. I was so worried about his reaction, his disappointment, and then ultimately his anger, that would surely come.

That evening, thankfully, he didn't come home until 7:00 p.m. When he got home, I let him eat dinner first and I tried to be calm. But, in truth, I was tied up in knots inside. My hands were visibly shaking.... I thought I was going to throw up. Finally, we were both in the living room when I decided to let him know about his results. I felt like I was delivering a death sentence. And for him, it definitely was.

"Hon, I have to talk to you about something important. I saw Dr. Suarez today." I was playing with my hands. I couldn't even look at him. I couldn't even stand up; my legs were shaking so badly. He noted my serious tone and his look was apprehensive. My eyes were already watering with tears. I was trying so hard to control myself. But it was too much for me. And as a result, he jumped to the wrong conclusion. He ran over to me and knelt down beside me and asked me what she said. "What is it hon? She found something wrong with you?" I responded, "Yes and no. Something is wrong with both of us." At that point he stood up, towering over me. I suddenly got up too. I wanted to get close to him to lessen the impact of the news I was about to deliver, but he didn't let me. He knew what I was going to say, of course.

"Clari, just tell me what she said about me." There was no way to soften this news.

"Your sperm count results came back. She said the results showed a low sperm count." "How low?" I was hoping he wouldn't ask me that. "She said you practically have no count." He suddenly turned around. He looked angry and hurt. "What do you mean?" "I mean you can't get me pregnant." The look of utter shock was unbearable. I searched his face for, I don't know what. All I wanted to do was hold him and make his pain go away. I went toward him, and he stopped me. "Please don't," he said to me. The look on his face was one that I never saw in the five years that I knew him. It was cold and hard. Then I said the wrong thing.

"She said that when the time was right, we should see a male infertility physician to find out more. She could recommend one for us. Or, I could do research." "Is she saying that I am sterile?" "Well, she never used that word, Edwin. You need to see a specialist to find out more." He then said something to me that really made me feel so awful for him and for us. He came really close to me and in a threatening whisper said to me, "Listen to me very carefully. I don't want to discuss my problem with anyone. Right now, I don't want to see anyone, and I don't want to hear anything more about having a baby. As you can see, I can't get you pregnant. So now we know, and we don't have to worry about that anymore. You are not to inform any member of my family nor your family about my problem. If they should ask, you tell them something else."

I pleaded, "Please, let's talk about this Edwin, please don't shut me out." Then he said, with the saddest look I had ever seen on his face, "I don't want to discuss it." He got up and left me alone in the living room. I cried for a long time and remembered Dr. Suarez' words about patience and understanding. Several hours later, I got up and took a bath and said a silent prayer. "God please, please help me through this."

The next couple of days at home were quiet. I tried to act normal. I knew the anger was going to come. I was preparing myself for it. One evening, it finally came - like a freight train. Edwin suddenly stood up in the living room and started talking at me, not to me. "How many times have we read in the newspapers about people who have babies and kill them or abort them? Here we are, two loving people, and we can't have them. I am being punished by God. That's what this is."

His words frightened me. I strongly believed in God. I replied in a whisper, almost hoping that God didn't hear him, "Don't speak like that, Edwin. You speak as if there may not be a solution. We could see someone and find out more." Then he yelled and screamed about the injustice being done to him.

"I am a good person and I don't deserve this, and God is punishing me! Why me?!" He started to cry. "There are sons of bitches out there who don't deserve to be fathers and yet they have babies left and right. Why me?" When I tried to go near him, he just pushed me away. Well, I was glad that he at least voiced his anger. Then he said, "Why did you have to do this? I wish you never had to find out why you couldn't get pregnant!"

He was blaming me now. I felt so guilty. I was openly crying too, but he didn't care. He finally went to our room and closed the door. I could hear him crying. I felt so bad and mad at myself. Maybe I should have left it alone. I started beating myself up about it.

I decided later that evening that I just had to give him time to deal with his pain. And in the meantime, I would try to love him and keep him happy. I didn't have to worry about the rhythm method any more. That was a relief. So, we could make love any time. I tried to look on the positive side of things. I loved him so very much.

Chapter 4:

New Hope

1982

During the next two years, Edwin concentrated on his second master's degree and I concentrated on my undergraduate studies for my BA degree. I had taken a year off when I got married. My thyroid condition was now under control. I learned that I would have to take Synthroid for the rest of my life, but I could now get pregnant, all things being equal of course.

Clari Diaz

When we weren't in school or at work, we traveled often to Florida, and in 1981, we went to Hawaii. Edwin finished his second master's degree in educational administration. He was teaching in an elementary school and wanted to be an Assistant Principal. In the meantime, my boss was offered a new job at Mount Sinai in Manhattan and he took me with him. I began earning a little more money and had a higher position. I was still going to undergraduate school at night. I only had one more year left!

One day, Edwin came home very excited. "Babe, you will never guess who I bumped into today!" I said, "Tell me!" Then he said, "I bumped into Eddie. He and his wife just had a baby boy." Eddie was Edwin's best friend when they were kids. They grew up together on 105th Street on the East side of Manhattan. They went to elementary and high school together. But, that was not the incredible news. He excitedly continued with his fantastic news, "Babe, you have to sit down." So, I did. "Eddie told me that he had a low sperm count and had an operation that helped him. He invited us to come over this weekend. He said he would talk to me more about his procedure and give us the name of the urology specialist."

I was excited and scared for him all at the same time. I didn't want to be negative, but what if the outcome was not positive, given the very low count. Then, all of the sudden, all my

44

bottled-up feelings surfaced. I had a lot of questions, like, now that he bumped into his childhood friend, it was suddenly "all right" to talk about having a baby? Never mind that he shut me out for two years. I tried to be understanding. Heck, I didn't know how the hell to feel. So, we had an argument.

"Let me try to understand you. You come home all excited because you bumped into Eddie, who had a low sperm count and had an operation and as a result was able to get his wife pregnant. Is this correct?" Then, he reacted to me. "You're upset."

"Yes, I am angry because you never wanted to discuss this, nor did you want me to pursue any options about learning more about male infertility, even though I work in a large medical center. You don't talk to me about your feelings. Most of all, you never even cared to ask how I felt." I was crying now.

"You are right, I didn't care. I was really upset and feeling sorry for myself. Here I am with a good job, a great wife and wonderful family and I can't have children. It is so damn unfair. Look, I didn't even think there was hope. Now, I know for sure that there is hope for me and I am excited about it. So, help me with this."

"Edwin, you know I will. Haven't I already shown you how much I care by giving you the space you needed."

"You have in every way." So, we made up that night and our love making was very intense, filled with so much emotion and passion. I was thrilled, I had my old Edwin back.

That weekend, we went to visit his friend. Edwin was so excited. We both played with the baby and he and his friend had some private time while I spoke with his wife. The next couple of weeks were filled with doctor appointments and lots of hope. We went to see the Urology specialist recommended by his friend Eddie. The first visit was a consultation. After the consult, Edwin agreed to return with a sperm sample. We received a call from the Urology specialist who indicated that Edwin had a chance of elevating his count. He was ecstatic and so was I.

Edwin agreed to undergo a Varicocelectomy, which is the most common operation performed for male infertility. When successful, it can result in an improved sperm count for men with this infertility problem. I kept my fingers crossed. But, I had a very strong premonition that this was not going to work. I tried to shut out those feelings, but I couldn't. I was scared for both of us. After several weeks, we found ourselves in the urologist's office waiting for the specialist to tell him if his sperm count was higher. When I saw the seriousness on the doctor's face, I knew the operation wasn't successful. The doctor gave it to us straight, "I am really sorry, the procedure did not elevate the sperm count high enough to have an impact in a pregnancy. You both should consider other means." Then he turned to me and suggested that I contact his colleague who is a GYN physician specializing in female infertility. That was it. I was terrified Edwin was going to shut down again. But to my immense surprise, he didn't. And, he surprised me when he was willing to let me pursue other options.

1983

We decided to concentrate on trying to get me pregnant by other means. For the next two years, I tried artificial insemination and taking hormone injections to make me more fertile. Every month, I would go to the doctor's office, where she inserted the sperm and then I had to lay with my legs up for 20 minutes. In the first year, when this didn't work, my GYN physician did a culdoscopy, which was similar to a scraping of my insides to see what was going on around my ovaries and uterus. After this procedure was done, she felt confident that I would be pregnant in three months. So, I went back on the hormone injections and went through artificial insemination again. But I couldn't get pregnant. All the tests they did always came back negative. There was nothing wrong with me physically. I was just infertile. I suddenly understood my husband's feelings. I felt so sad for us both. My GYN physician was never able to diagnose my infertility, which was totally frustrating and provided very little hope in becoming pregnant.

1985

At the medical center where I worked, I started to hear the buzz about IVF: In-Vitro Fertilization. In IVF, eggs are gathered from the woman's ovaries and mixed with the man's sperm outside the body, usually in a glass dish in a laboratory. "In vitro" comes from Latin and literally means "in glass," a reference to the glass container where fertilization of the egg (oocyte) takes place. (While this is usually a dish, the term "test-tube babies" has become widely used.) The fertilized eggs are then cultivated for two or three days to embryo stage and transferred to the woman's uterus. So, I decided to see the IVF specialist at Mount Sinai, where I worked. He was very positive, and he had a nice warm demeanor. His office was surrounded by pictures of babies. I hoped a picture of my baby would join his wall of fame. It gave me a positive feeling. We talked to him about our infertility and felt very positive about getting me pregnant. We were excited because we could use Edwin's sperm. No more artificial insemination! Edwin felt really good about this, as well. He wanted us to go to an introductory seminar where IVF was explained in detail so we could begin to understand each phase of this complicated process.

We decided to go through with IVF after the meeting. The procedure sounded hopeful, although it would be very demanding and stressful for me. I had to take drugs to suppress my own hormones. This phase lasts about twenty-one days. The drugs have the effect of putting the body into a temporary low hormone state (similar to a short-term menopause), along with all of the side effects that might be expected such as hot flashes and mood swings. After the hormones were suppressed, I began taking the medication that would stimulate the ovaries and egg production. Edwin had to learn how to give me injections on my butt, which he did daily for eight to twelve days.

Normally, a woman produces one egg in each menstrual cycle. But with IVF, many ovarian follicles are produced by hormone stimulation and several eggs are obtained (usually 7-15). By the end of a two-month cycle, I was irritable, and my butt was black and blue from all the injections. The response of the ovaries was carefully monitored using ultrasound scanning to show the size and number of developing follicles and frequent blood tests were also performed.

Finally, the time came to remove the eggs that I produced. On the night before removal of the eggs, I had to drink two cups of tea or coffee and go to bed. I decided to drink the tea. I was not allowed to urinate. I had to be at the hospital at 7:00 a.m. and Edwin had to be in another room to submit a sperm sample. Well, I didn't think I was going to make it to the hospital. I was walking like a baby who had soiled her underpants. My ovaries felt like hard marbles on both sides of my bladder, considering all the water I was holding in. They finally did the sonogram. As the technician pressed the scope over my abdomen, I had to concentrate hard not to urinate. My bladder was about to explode. The doctor confirmed at last that I had not ovulated and counted thirteen eggs. I yelled out, "Holy shit!" Everyone in the room started to laugh.

I was finally told I could urinate and I thought I was going to be on the toilet for hours. It was endless, since I just don't pee fast! The nurse kept on knocking on the door because, at any second, I could ovulate. Then, I started to laugh. It must have been comic relief from all the strain. I finally hopped on the table. I was given anesthesia and I felt I could relax, at last. The eggs were collected using a fine, hollow needle guided by ultrasound.

When the anesthesia wore off, I felt my lower extremities shaking badly. The nurse came over and put a warm blanket on me. She whispered in my ear, "Your husband is in the room next door right now." I had a smile on my face.

Edwin's sperm was assessed and prepared for fertilization. As soon as the eggs were extracted, they were placed into a nutrient "embryo culture" medium with the sperm and then placed in an incubator overnight. The next day, the eggs were observed through a microscope to see if fertilization has occurred. Edwin fertilized five eggs. The next day, cell division started, and the embryo would have two or four cells. The embryos were checked by the embryologist to ensure that they were developing normally and, if all was well, embryo transfer could take place. We were called back to the hospital for the embryo transfer. Three out of the five developed normally and together with a tiny amount of nutrient fluid, were put into a catheter and placed into my uterus through my cervix with a special ultrasound guidance.

That evening Edwin and I had to have intercourse in order to provide the right environment for the embryos, according to my physician. The doctor felt that his sperm would nurture the embryos. But intercourse was very difficult, since my abdomen was sore. He didn't want to hurt me, and I had to grit my teeth through the whole thing, because I had stitches inside and outside my abdomen. I couldn't see how this was nurturing with all the pain. But we did as we were told. The next day, I walked around the house like I was carrying precious cargo. I held my abdomen as I walked around, hoping my hands would help them thrive. I didn't want to pee for fear of anything slipping out. I sat with my feet up and tried to think positive thoughts. During this time, I was prescribed progesterone, which is needed to provide hormonal support in case of pregnancy.

After about two weeks, I had to go back for a blood test that would reveal if I was pregnant. I didn't feel any different and I didn't think I was. I knew my body too damn well, even with all the drugs and medication I had been given. I was supposed to call for my results. But instead, the doctor called to see us. My husband and I went into his office, hoping for positive results. But the news was not good. The doctor was very kind and wanted us try again in three months.

Instead, we returned in six months and tried again. The doctor changed the hormones a little the second time around and I could give myself the injections in my thigh this time. That was much better, and I didn't have to yell at Edwin all the time. But knowing everything I had to go through all over again made this cycle of IVF unbearable.

These hormones were much stronger, and I once again became very irritable. In the end, I produced thirteen eggs again and endured the process of removing the eggs and transplantation. He fertilized five again and this time they all thrived! We decided to go with three and hold two in reserve. It was fine as far as I was concerned. When I went home, the physician didn't want us to have intercourse. He just wanted me to be calm and to rest with my feet up and not do anything strenuous. I once again followed doctor's orders.

Several weeks later, we were back in the doctor's office. By the look on the doctor's face, I knew we didn't succeed. He wanted to try again. He urged us to return in three months. The doctor wanted to transplant the two frozen embryos. I agreed. It would be less stressful, and no procedure was involved. He felt that this might actually work.

I endured the injections once again, but this time, my eggs would not be removed. My doctor wanted us to have intercourse during ovulation. The doctor felt that anything was possible. But the hormones really started to take their toll on me. This time I was going through a lot of crying and became a little depressed through the process. Edwin was worried. Finally, the time came for the transplant, but I was not feeling positive mentally. It was too much. In the end, I didn't get pregnant. We were both upset, and I had had enough! I couldn't do this anymore. I didn't want any more injections or procedures done on me any longer.

I decided to give myself and Edwin some breathing space. No more doctors, no more injections, and no more talking about IVF or trying to get pregnant. Over the summer, we took a ten-day vacation to California. We stayed in

San Francisco for three days. Then we boarded a bus to take a ride around the Big Sur to Los Angeles. We stopped at several points of interest along the way. We walked around a lot and held each other and got back to loving each other for no reason other than sheer pleasure. It was what we both needed to heal and reconnect as a couple. Our friends and family all felt that now that we were relaxed, I would get pregnant. But I didn't want to think or talk about getting pregnant.

Chapter 5:

A New Beginning

In 1986, we were in our eighth year of our marriage. After I let some time pass, I still had that ache for wanting a child. However, I no longer had the incredible need to have my own. One night I spoke to Edwin about what I was thinking.

"Honey, when you first learned about your infertility, you said that you were being punished by God. First of all, God doesn't punish us. We do that to ourselves. I feel that everything in life happens for a reason. What if our purpose is not to have our own child, but to give a child a loving home? I think we should look into adopting a baby. How do you feel about that for us?"

Edwin looked at me and said, "Let's speak to my sister about it." Edwin's sister and her husband were adoptive parents and they had adopted two babies many years before. So, we went to talk to his sister, Iris, to gain insight on the prospect of us becoming adoptive parents, as well.

After talking to Iris, she suggested we speak to an adoption agency in Westchester County that she heard about. When we did, the woman we spoke with was not very friendly. She was very matter of fact. It felt like we were applying for a loan. The woman simply gave us some information to read and an application to complete and indicated that adoption for an infant could take five or more years. She didn't sound encouraging. I didn't even bother filling out the application. I was completely turned off by the woman's standoffish manner.

After a while, I thought, why not try to adopt from Puerto Rico? Edwin and I are both first generation Puerto Rican Americans. But, when I inquired, I learned from the Department of Health in Puerto Rico that we had to establish residency for a minimum of six months. Therefore, it was quite impossible to pursue this option, as our parents lived here in New York and there was simply no way of getting around the residency issue. Both Edwin and I did not want to involve any relatives from Puerto Rico on this very private matter.

I then looked into New York City adoption agencies, thinking about single young women who might want to give up their baby for adoption, due to social-economic conditions or other factors, and at the same time, hoping to increase our chances for a Hispanic baby. However, twenty years ago, the City's Agencies' main objective was to rehabilitate the birth mother. Families interested in adopting would have to become foster parents first, and bring the infant to the agencies for visitation by the birth mother during the rehabilitation period. During this time, the foster parents could apply for adoption of the infant in their care. However, a certain amount of time had to pass, and a great deal of legal paperwork needed to be submitted that would release the infant for adoption. And, there was always the possibility that the birth mother could take the infant back if her situation improved, or if the biological father objected to the adoption. We, as adopting parents, would have no rights whatsoever. The baby could be taken away from us. I couldn't see myself taking on a role as a foster parent first. This kind of uncertainty, where at any time the baby might be taken away from me, would simply break my heart. I was not willing to take this risk and put my family and the child in my care through this trauma.

I then looked into other adoption agencies like Spence-Chapin, but the waiting time for an infant was ambiguous. Every avenue I looked into had huge obstacles. At this point, I felt like it was completely hopeless. We would never be able to have a baby of our own.

My sixth sense was not revealing anything to me at all. I was in the dark. The reason I was in the dark was because I never, ever asked God for his help. I went to church, but I had stopped talking to God. I was so consumed by trying to have a baby that I never entered into prayer for guidance. I was flying solo. But, unbeknownst to me, a door was about to open. God was watching over me in his own way.

One day in September at work, one of our nurses came to visit. She was holding a baby boy of about five months. She had taken a personal leave of absence. No one in the office knew about her situation. All the women in the office, including me, crowded around her. "Who is this beautiful baby boy?" Well she said, "This is my son, I just adopted him from El Salvador. I learned about international adoptions from a close friend and found out that El Salvador allowed single people to adopt from their country." She was not married. She indicated that the adoption took a long time. She had gone to El Salvador three months earlier to see her baby and fill out some paperwork, and then she had to come back and wait for her lawyer to call her and let her know when she had to appear before the court to make the adoption final and bring her baby home. "I just got back two weeks ago and today, I decided to bring my baby in so everyone could meet him." What a blessing, I thought to myself. I was in awe of the baby and of her. She looked absolutely radiant.

I was so excited and itching to have an opportunity to speak to her alone. After she visited with everyone, I kindly asked her if she wouldn't mind speaking to me in private. We went into the conference room, which thankfully was empty. I thanked her right away. "Thank you for letting me speak to you in private. My husband and I have been looking into adopting for a while and I never heard of international adoption. Would you mind sharing how we can learn about international adoptions?"

She happily replied, "Actually, I found out about international adoption from another nurse who adopted from Colombia. She put me in touch with an organization called LAPA. Here, I have a brochure in my bag. They are not an adoption agency. LAPA is a parent-help group that provides individuals and couples with information about adoptions from Latin American. All they ask for is a $20.00 membership fee. Every month they have an adoption workshop. Call the number on the brochure and find out the date of the next workshop. You can pay for the membership fee before you go into the meeting. Listen I have to go now, but I know this organization will help you. But you must have perseverance, Clari. It will not be easy."

I could barely say thank you. I was in shock. I couldn't wait to talk to Edwin about this new lead. I immediately called the number on the form. I found out that within three weeks they were conducting an adoption workshop. I jotted down the date, time and place.

When Edwin got home, I told him I had exciting news. He, however, wasn't so excited. After I finished telling him about LAPA, his response was, "International adoption? I don't know about this, Hon. We don't know anything about international adoption." He looked really worried. I had to talk fast before he completely shut me down. "Edwin look, this month, LAPA is having an adoption workshop. Let's go together and find out what they have to say. It will only cost us $20 and little of our time. That is not very much. Please say yes."

He saw the look of pleading on my face. "I know you will not take no for an answer, so we will go, but please, let's listen first and not make any impulsive decisions." I agreed. I was so happy. I knew I was going to be restless until that day came. I just couldn't wait to go. My heart filled with joy and hope once again.

Well, the day finally came. It felt endless just waiting, and even more endless to finally get there. I remember calling that morning to make sure they hadn't canceled the meeting. The workshop was going to take place as scheduled. I was so very excited. I could barely concentrate on work.

When we got to the workshop, I was amazed at the number of other families present. Edwin was, as well. The meeting was held in a school cafeteria in Long Island and the place was completely full of people. In fact, folks who arrived late had to stand. We were both expecting a small group of people. We had no idea that there were so many like-minded people who were interested in adopting, and astonishingly, looking to adopt from Latin American.

The meeting started with a woman greeting everyone and talking about her adoption experience in Brazil. In the middle of her story, a little voice from the back the room yelled out, "I love you mommy." We all turned to see her young two-year-old son sitting on the shoulders of his daddy. It was so endearing to see this display of emotion from her young son and her response to him as well. All the couples in the room had the same expression on their faces. This is what we came here to see, witness, and confirm, that at the end of this precious journey, we would have a child of our own.

After the talks were over, we were given an adoption packet to take home. The information the packet contained was overwhelming. The packet included lists of various adoption sources from countries in Latin American, a list of lawyers in New York, as well as in Latin America, a list of social workers, a list of licensed translators, immigration information, immigration forms and general information about the adoption process outside the United States, and a member directory. I read through all the material several times, trying to comprehend this enormous, complicated process.

Several days later, Edwin and I sat to talk about the workshop. We put the packet in front of us and we decided to take the first step and get a Home Study done. A Home Study is the first document adoptive parents must obtain which indicates information about their family background, education, religious beliefs, marriage and their professional life....in essence, the details of our whole life up to the present, on paper.

About two weeks later, we had an appointment to see a Social Worker. I had made some phone calls to a few of the LAPA members that I found in my packet and decided to go with a Social Worker that lived in Old Westbury, New York who came highly recommended. I was told by one of the members that she had a disability. Her name was Miriam Vienni. I didn't know her disability, until she brought us upstairs to her office and I saw the Braille typewriter. Miriam was legally blind. Miriam knew a great deal about international adoption. She was warm and put us at ease immediately. She informed us that she adopted a little girl from China many years ago. Her daughter was now a teenager. Throughout the entire intake process, Miriam was comforting, sympathetic, humorous and most of all encouraging, which was what we needed most. She also provided a wealth of information in relation to the adoption process and advised me to create a family history on every member of our immediate family. She noted that some Latin American countries like to see that. I jotted this down in my notes and everything else she shared with us.

After we received the Home Study, Edwin and I sat down again to look at the countries. We crossed out the ones that didn't meet our criteria. We wanted to adopt an infant. Some countries offered adoptions for older children. We circled two sources, both from Colombia. One source only dealt with couples of the Catholic faith. The only problem was that I had to stay for a period of two months. The other one didn't offer much information, aside from indicating that adoption for an infant was possible. So, we decided it was time to talk to our parents about our plans.

My father was clearly upset. I was his only daughter and child and the thought of going to a foreign country to adopt a baby was beyond his comprehension. He wanted me to pray and ask God for help. "He will provide." My response was, "Dad, I love you and I don't mean any disrespect. Everything in life happens for a reason. I think this is our fate, to give a child a loving home." He replied, "I understand, but why do you have to go so far to adopt. Why can't you adopt from here or even Puerto Rico?" He was scared for us both. He wanted to know all the details. I sat down and explained to him that we had exhausted all those other possibilities. After an hour of talking to dad, he finally gave us his blessing, but he was apprehensive. Privately, I then asked my mother if she wouldn't mind staying with me in a foreign country when the time came, because Edwin didn't want to leave me alone. He couldn't stay for two months. She told me she would discuss it with dad. Oh God, he won't be happy, was my thought upon leaving mom.

In the meantime, I quietly interviewed every member of my immediate family. I felt like a journalist, writing down all their personal information about their lives. It was very interesting, and it became a special time for all of us, including my dad, who I loved a great deal.

My folder on adoption was growing. I had to reorganize all the documents. I started separating all the documents into categories and setting up separate folders for everything:

- Home Study
- Immigration Information and Forms

- Adoption Sources and Phone Numbers
- Our Marriage Certificate
- Our Birth Certificates
- Family History
- Lawyers
- Social Workers
- Verification of Employment
- LAPA Information
- Licensed Translators
- Medical History
- Letters of Reference
- Psychological Report

I was a woman with a mission. Edwin left me to handle everything. He was busy with his job that totally consumed him. He was going on lots of interviews to become an assistant principal.

Now that we spoke to our parents, the next step was to inquire about the source from Colombia. I called a LAPA member to find out more about the agency we chose. I was given a phone number of another LAPA member who was directly involved with this agency. I also called my Social Worker to find out what she knew about the source.

My social worker was very encouraging and had positive things to say about the source and the LAPA member. So, I called her and left a message. When I received the return phone call, I explained that I was at a LAPA workshop recently and that my husband and I were interested in finding out more about this source. She indicated that she helped couples from the Catholic faith adopt from this agency. She asked if we were Catholic and I said "Yes." She was having a meeting at her house at the end of week and she invited us to join a group. We went to the meeting and met other couples. Everyone was excited, just like us.

The woman, whose name I really don't remember, described the adoption process in Colombia. She listed the forms to complete with immigration before going to Colombia, and the type of other documents required by the agency. She let us know that once all the documents were done, they had to be notarized and authenticated at the County Clerk's office. Then the documents had to be translated into Spanish by a licensed translator. I raised my hand. "Excuse me, but I speak and write Spanish. Couldn't I do this?"

"No. The courts in Latin America must see a seal on the document verifying that it was translated by a licensed translator. After this is accomplished, you must take the documents to the Colombian Consulate for their seal of approval. They are very familiar with the process. It will take a few days and they will call you and let you know when to pick up your documents."

I raised my hand again. "Excuse me, what is your role in this process?" She smiled. "Look, all this information is very overwhelming when you first hear about all the documents you have to get. But is it doable. My role is to take your documents and send them to the agency. I assure the agency that I reviewed the documents and verify that I met with each of you in person. This agency is very careful and wants to be sure that the infant is being placed with loving, responsible parents that are from the Catholic faith. I will contact you if the agency needs any additional documents and I will also contact you when you have to go to Colombia. I will help you make the hotel reservations and provide additional information as you get near to the adoption."

She then told us that she was an adoptive parent herself. "I am not going to put my children on display. I must caution you. I tell this to every couple that wants to adopt a child from Latin America. The child is not going to resemble you." I naturally felt that since we were of Hispanic origin, the child would somehow resemble us. But, she was completely correct. And, like a mosquito that annoys you, I simply swatted what she said from my mind.

"So, the next step for you is to call me when you have all your documents ready. If I have any information, I will call you." We each gave her our names, addresses and phone numbers.

Edwin was overwhelmed with all the documentation that was needed. I, on the other hand, was having a strong premonition. We were not going to adopt from this agency. However, I learned a lot and there was a lot of work still to be done. I silently prayed that my fears would not come true. I should know better by now, shouldn't I?

About three months later, I received a phone call from the woman we visited about the adoption from Colombia. She had sad news to report. "Clari, the agency shut down." I asked what happened. She indicated that some political issues came up about this agency that would not allow people from the United States to adopt from them. If it should re-open, she would call, but she didn't think it would. She advised that I look for another source. I asked if she could recommend one. "No, you should go to another adoption workshop to see if there are any new sources. The organization updates the lists for each workshop." I was so upset. But, I was not surprised. I didn't feel positive. I almost wanted to curse these premonitions because they were never false. But, of course, I didn't. For me they were a gift.

I called my Social Worker who was always so kind and helpful. She had the same suggestion. "Clari, go to the next adoption workshop. Maybe you will learn something new." My enthusiasm was not the same when we went to the next workshop. There were very few additions and no other sources similar to the Colombian source. After reviewing the sources again, with a very heavy heart, I eventually selected another organization in Colombia. However, this source was totally different. We were on our own with this adoption agency. The information indicated that the couples had to write directly to the agency in Colombia. I wrote to them requesting an application and asking what documents they required from us and if they could provide additional information concerning the adoption process. I started a new folder.

I received an answer a month later informing us that they accepted our application and the agency listed all the documents they needed. I had some of the documents already. It was a new beginning and I felt elated once again. However, after two months passed, I had heard nothing. I wrote to them again and they indicated that the waiting for an infant could take a very long time. Six months turned into a year with no word from the adoption agency in Colombia, only various letters indicating that we had to be patient. As I recall this time in my life, I remember how down I felt. I knew that I needed to look for another source. This agency was simply not going to come through for us.

Clari Diaz

Chapter 6:

Faith

1987

The next series of events took place a year later, in 1987. Edwin had become the Bilingual Coordinator at his school and I was still working full-time at Mount Sinai in Manhattan. I had a new boss that liked me a great deal. We were both doing well in our respective careers. I had already finished my undergraduate studies and obtained my BA degree. My studies helped me cope through the strain of trying to adopt. Edwin and I were both very family oriented and the added plus of having our loving and supportive parents living in the same neighborhood helped us get through this difficult time.

On weekends, my parents would often come by and pick me up to go shopping or see family. My parents always called me to see what I was doing so I wouldn't be home alone to mope. I didn't drive much back then, only on the weekends when Edwin let me have the car to go to the mall in New Rochelle to window shop. Edwin tutored, which kept him busy on the weekends.

Early one Saturday morning in March, I was alone at home and I just hit rock bottom emotionally. I started to weep uncontrollably and collapsed alongside my bed. I laid still for the longest time with dried up tears on my face. Suddenly, I felt like someone was holding me and I began my conversation with God. Very softly, I said, "God, I need your help. Please look on me with mercy. I know that with your divine intervention all things are possible. I tried as best as I can to find a child that could benefit from our love. But all we find are obstacles." I started crying again. I was on my knees for a long time and then just stayed kneeling and became calm when the following words just came out of me. "God, I know that You know that there is a little girl out there for me that needs me. Please help me find her. I leave this petition in Your hands. Please do as You will. I am and always will be your devoted servant. Amen." This inspirational moment suddenly produced a realization that revealed, without a doubt, that I would never conceive a child of my own, but that God was going to lead me to my little girl. I can't explain how I knew this, but I did. When I finally got up from my knees an hour later, I felt relieved, inspired, and free of my tormented thoughts.

In the month of July of that same year, someone knocked on our door at home. It was my husband's dear cousin, Izzy. Izzy was also a school teacher for New York City, like Edwin, and they often shared many humorous stories about their students and colleagues. When we got together, it always felt like a wonderful family reunion. We would always part saying that we needed to get together more often, but our busy everyday lives got in the way of that need to reunite. When he arrived, we were so genuinely happy to see him, it was a very pleasant surprise for us both. As I opened the door, I exclaimed, "Oh Izzy, what a surprise! Who died?" He started to laugh a little and said, "I know this is a shock to see me at your door. My mom is here in Coop visiting with your parents Edwin and I thought I would surprise you both. Actually, I didn't expect to find you two at home on such a beautiful day. How come you guys are home?"

I responded for both of us. "Well Izzy you know we are a little down in the dumps due to the adoption issue."

"Well if I may ask.... what is going on with that?"

I answered by saying, "Truthfully, it is nowhere right now. We have not heard from the adoption agency in Colombia in months and we know we have to look for a new source. But I haven't done so yet." Then he said the oddest thing, "I would like to help you two." Understanding all I knew about international adoption, I didn't quite comprehend how he could help. I asked, "Do you know a lawyer?" He simply answered, "No, I plan to put the word out in my church. Just give me six months?" I agreed thinking within myself that he was just trying to be helpful and kind, not realizing that God had sent me an angel. Izzy stayed with us into the late afternoon and then left to pick up his mom.

They say that God works in mysterious ways. And, the next series of events proved that you just have to have faith. Izzy was true to his word. In late November of 1987, he telephoned. I happened to be home alone. "Clari, it's Izzy. I have some amazing news!"

"What?" I said.

He answered, "Pack your bags, you're going to Paraguay." My heart simply dropped to my knees and I had to find a chair before I fell down as my legs started to tremble. I felt dizzy, as well. "What? What is going on Izzy? You are scaring me. Start again." He was laughing a little at my reaction.

"Are you sitting down?"

"I am now because I think my feet won't hold me."

"Clari, I spoke to my neighbor Susan. I know her and her husband well and her daughter goes to school with my Rebecca. Since Susan is from Colombia, I thought she might know someone. Well, she did. She spoke to her neighbors, Persio and Blanca who are from Paraguay. They have two teenage kids. Persio contacted his sister and brother-in-law in Paraguay, who told him they would be willing to help you guys and want you to go to Paraguay right away." I was speechless. "Hello, Clari?" Finally, my brain cells started to function again.

"Izzy, listen to me. It's just not that simple. Who are these people? Did you meet Persio and Blanca?" He said yes that he met Persio and his wife and spoke to them directly. I took a deep breath and explained that adopting from Latin America is complicated and as a result I simply could not just drop everything and go because certain documents needed to be filed at Immigration in New York and a great deal of documents had to be sent to Paraguay for the courts. Also, no matter what Izzy was saying to me, my survival instincts as a New Yorker were heightened and I immediately thought this was a scam of some sort. I started to question these people's motives. Izzy tried to put me at ease and told me these were hard working people of the

Catholic faith like us and simply want to help us. He explained that I could count on his judgment in assessing someone's character and motive.

"Izzy, nothing is going to happen until we have a meeting of all the families." That sounded like a scene right out of the *Godfather* movie, but nevertheless a true statement. "Talk to Persio and Blanca and your friend, Susan and your wife, Maria, and find out when everyone can come to my house for dinner, like next weekend for example." Izzy then said, "That is actually a great idea. I will call you in a few days." I was also planning to invite my parents and Edwin's parents, too. There is power in numbers, and I really needed my family around me for this dinner.

Izzy called back in three days and the dinner was set for the weekend, which was in the first week of December. I was very excited, but apprehensive. The night of the dinner, Edwin and I were both very excited and exchanged family stories before then starting to talk about our desire to adopt a baby. By the time the evening was over, Persio took me aside and spoke to me privately in Spanish. "Mrs. Clari, this is my sister Elvira's number in Paraguay and my number in New York. Her husband's name is Angel Ruiz Diaz. Call them tomorrow around 8:00 p.m. They will be expecting your call and let me know what happens, so I can help you in any way I can."

"Thank you, Persio. You know, I am a little nervous. Are you sure that they can help us? He said, "I know they can. That is all I can tell you right now. You just have to trust them."

I spoke to Edwin and we decided to follow through with the phone call. I actually couldn't wait until the next day to contact Elvira and Angel. I spoke Spanish fluently. I remember dialing the number slowly, making sure I didn't make a mistake. I waited anxiously for the call to go through, which felt like an eternity. Elvira's husband answered the phone. "Hello, this is Clari calling from New York. Your brother-in-law, Persio gave me your number."

"Senora Clari, yes Persio told me you would be calling me this evening. My name is Angel Ruiz Diaz and I am Elvira's husband. Persio is her brother. You can talk to me." Okay, I thought to myself. I remember, his manner was one of warmth and very cordial. Then he started the conversation. "Persio told me that you are interested in adopting a baby from Paraguay."

"Yes, my husband and I have been married for eleven years and we cannot have a baby of our own for medical reasons."

"Why do you want a baby from Paraguay? Why can't you adopt from North America?"

I explained, "It is very difficult to adopt from here for many legal reasons. The process is complicated and there is no assurance that the adopted baby would be ours. We tried to do this, but it is not easy to do. We also tried to adopt from Puerto Rico, but I have to actually reside in Puerto Rico to adopt and both our parents live here in New York. Could you help us?"

"I would like to meet you and your husband in person if that is possible." "Anything is possible Mr. Diaz."

"Please call me Angel."

"Angel, for us to go to Paraguay right now, my husband and I would have to request a leave. He is a teacher and I work in a hospital. It is not easy for us to get time off because we know we have to request this time when we actually have to go before the courts to adopt the baby. Why don't I send you my documents and you can read them and let me know what you think? I will need an adoption lawyer from your country, eventually."

Angel responded, "I fully understand what you are saying. Yes, I agree that is a good start. Send your documents to me." I felt it was important for him to know how long it would take to get my documents to him. So, I told him, "Angel, please be patient. It will take a week because I have to have them stamped by the Paraguayan Consulate's office." He understood and said, "Very well, call me when you are ready to send them." I hung up and still didn't really know who he was, and I felt that I just had to be patient. He was being cautious as well.

I had a huge task ahead of me. I had made a second set of originals just in case, a suggestion from my social worker, Miriam. I had the documents notarized and authenticated by the County Clerk's office where the notary was registered. The documents were already translated into Spanish and the final step was to take them to the Consulate of Paraguay for approval. There were actually twenty-one documents in total. These documents represented our whole lives on paper. I learned that the Consulate's office was in the World Trade Center II, on the 92nd floor, and I had to leave them. I was told by the clerk that in three to four days, I could pick them up. I had to call them. How ironic that when I dropped them off, I thought, "What if something went wrong?" But then I thought, "What could possibly go wrong in this huge building?" There was no way I could know that, several years later, tragedy would indeed strike the World Trade Centers.

When I left the documents at the consulate's office, I was beside myself with nerves. Just in case, I made copies of every single document. I walked around the basement at the World Trade Centers and bought my baby girl a knitted Christening outfit. In three days, I called, but I had to wait one more day. On the fourth day, I returned and picked up my documents and silently thanked God for their return and carried them securely. I felt like I was carrying the most precious gift.

I made a phone call to Angel that evening to let him know that the documents were being sent to him by DHL Courier Service. To say that I held my breath until those documents arrived in Paraguay was putting it mildly. Angel called me several days later to confirm that he had received them, and he promised to call me later in the week. I was finally able to breathe easier again. I don't know how I got through the waiting time. We were already in the third week of December and a lot had happened in such a short amount of time.

Angel phoned me about two days later. "Senora Clari."

"Angel please drop the Senora and just call me Clari." I could hear him laughing on the other end.

"Okay, like you like to say." It was my turn to laugh. Then he said, "Clari I was really moved by your family history. After reading everything, I want to tell you that I will move mountains to help you adopt a baby from my country. And I will now tell you who I am. I am a judge in this country, but now retired. I have already spoken to an adoption lawyer and he will be reviewing your documents and he will let me know if anything else is required by the courts. Leave the rest to me."

Then I said so gratefully, "Angel, I don't know what to say except God bless you for agreeing to help us."

"Don't worry about anything," he said. I thanked him once again and hung up. I realized at that point that nothing was going to happen to prevent me from having my little girl. A judge. I couldn't believe it! This was divine intervention at work. "Thank you, God, because only you make the impossible possible," were my thoughts. I felt so grateful.

I called Izzy and filled him in on the details and then I called Persio, as well, to let him know what had transpired with Angel. Of course, he already knew.

That same week, Angel telephoned again, and this time placed the attorney on the phone to speak to me. He told me that he reviewed my documents, but that he needed one more, which was a Certificate of Good Conduct. He then told me to submit it as quickly as I could manage. We spoke about his fee and he would accept payment from us when we arrived in Paraguay. I immediately called Miriam, my social worker, since I didn't know what this document was and at the same time brought her up-to-date on the new developments. She gave me a great deal of encouragement and informed me how to obtain the certificate the lawyer was requesting. It was a certificate produced by the local Police Department which verifies that there are no criminal records against us. Edwin and I needed to go down to the main Police Department at One Police Plaza in lower Manhattan and get ourselves finger printed for this document. Of course, this took another two weeks. We had to have the two certificates translated, notarized, authenticated and then signed by the Consulate of Paraguay, which meant another trip to the World Trade Center. By this time, it was the end of December when these last documents were sent to Angel.

Finally, everything was done. We were at the most crucial point in the adoption process and that was waiting for a phone call to tell us that we were going to be parents. During this time, my husband and I started "nesting." We lived in a three-bedroom apartment with two bathrooms. We painted the second bedroom in a pale lavender. I placed a beautiful border around the room. We purchased baby furniture and I started buying some baby clothes. I started crocheting a couple things, as well. I also read Dr. Spock for the *third* unbelievable time! I think I was literally trying to memorize the book. I was happy, scared, nervous, and stressed all at the same time.

Chapter 7:

My Gift

On January 8, 1988, I got a call from Persio at 10:00 p.m. at night. "What did you dream of last night?" was what he said to me after I said hello. I couldn't even speak. I was already in tears. Then he said, "Your daughter was born at 1 a.m. this morning." Did I hear him right? He did say "your daughter?" This was all going through my mind in split seconds as he was talking because I wasn't saying anything. Then he said, "You are now a mommy." I finally found my voice. Edwin was standing next to me as I spoke, "Persio, oh my God! Does Angel have her already? Do you know? Thank you for calling me. Where is Angel? Could I get a picture of her? What did she look like?"

I could tell he was smiling and laughing at my reaction as he spoke. "Angel is in the interior seeing to all the details. He wanted you to know right away about the baby's birth." Before he hung up, he promised to talk to Angel about a picture. I didn't know what to say or do when I hung up. I did want to fly out right away to see my little baby girl. But it was still too soon. It was a miracle. God found my little girl! We have a little girl......I was simply in awe of God, truly humbled by this wonderful gift I was given. I was a mommy. I couldn't believe it! Edwin and I hugged each other, and we decided not to tell anyone yet, until we got her picture. I was lost in thought that night and I knew, without any doubt, that nothing was going to go wrong with the adoption because God placed my daughter in a direct path to me. Nothing did go wrong, but the waiting time during the months that followed was the most difficult part of the whole adoption process to endure.

Actually, the word 'difficult' was putting it mildly. It was downright nerve-racking. Angel wanted me to come down in February and stay with them until the adoption was finalized. Angel then explained that the months of December and January are Paraguay's summer and the courts and schools close down during this time and don't reopen until February, so nothing was going to move until then. I also learned that his wife, Elvira, was a school teacher and there was no one to care for my baby girl when Elvira returned to work in February. I told him that I needed to discuss everything with my husband and I would phone him in a few days.

Edwin was really nervous, "I am not going to allow you to go to a foreign country, not knowing how long you have to stay. I will agree to one month, but we go together if we must." Also, there was the financial burden of being without a paycheck. We were saving every cent we made for this adoption. The roundtrip airfare alone was over $1,800 per person. He was right, of course, and I was nervous. I needed extra money and I didn't want to ask my parents. But, I felt I needed to ask for at least $1,000 to help us with some of the costs when we arrived in Paraguay.

Three days later, I phoned Angel, being careful with my words. I explained that in New York, during holiday time, we were not off. Our vacation time is earned vacation time. The schools and organizations don't close for two months like in Paraguay. I explained that we were saving our earned vacation time for when we would be bringing the baby home. If we took a leave of absence for a long period of time, we would not receive a salary. I let him know that I desperately wanted to be with the baby and meet his family. I told him that we were trying to see if

I could go down for a month. He understood perfectly, and he confirmed everything I was saying with his brother-in-law, Persio. The next day, he telephoned with the most unbelievable news. His wife, Elvira, would be able to take a leave of absence to take care of the baby for us. He indicated that we should save our time for when we had to go before the courts. I was speechless. I had no words to express my gratitude. A simple thank you paled in comparison to the sacrifice they were making for people they didn't even know. I told him I would send him clothes and wire money for any expenses that they needed for the baby. I realized that Elvira was stepping in as a foster parent on my behalf until it was time to bring my little girl home. I was worried about how long the process would take and how she was going to feel emotionally when it was time to give her over to me. Would she be able to give up my baby? The only consolation I had was that she already had two children of her own, Necky who was nine and Danny who was eleven. I was grateful and nervous all at the same time. Yet, deep inside, I knew that nothing was going to go wrong.

For four months, I kept busy getting ready for my baby girl. We decided to name her Marisa Sonia. Edwin picked out the first name. Initially, he wanted to name the baby Melissa, but I wanted a Spanish name. So, I said, "How about Marisa?" He said, "Marisa is pretty. I like it."

Then, I added Sonia, after my sister who passed away at the tender age of two.

While waiting for my baby's picture to arrive, I started fantasizing about what she would look like. I thought when her picture arrived, I would be alone in my home looking at her picture, memorizing her face, and having this private moment. I could cry, enjoy and envelope myself in this feeling of finally being a mommy. I totally, totally forgot about Edwin in this fantasy that I was developing in my mind. Every day, for what seemed an endless amount of time, I flew home from work to check the mail box. Well, as luck would have it, Edwin got to see the baby pictures first. He called me at work all excited telling me that we received the pictures. "Honey, we got her pictures today!" I responded excitedly, "We did? What does she look like?" He answered, "She is beautiful."

As he was talking to me, I could hear people talking in the background. So, I said, "Where are you?" And he responded, "I'm at my mother's house." I was simply stunned! All my raw emotions surfaced. "How could you do that! This was our special moment just for us. After all the planning, coordinating, and running around getting everything ready. This was our special moment only for us." I was upset because the special moment I had fantasized about didn't come the way I envisioned it. I felt suddenly unappreciated. What gave him the right to do this after all the pain I went through to this point? I admit, I was beyond hysterical. I totally lost it. Then he said to me, "Don't spoil this moment. And hurry to my mother's house." It was like he threw a cup of cold water on my face. So, I reacted. Edwin was right. He had a right to share this moment. I was being selfish. I was so ashamed. I just felt like the baby was all mine. So, when I arrived at my mother-in-law's house, to add insult to even more injury, there was my baby's picture starring up at me from the kitchen table and my reaction written all over my face. I said in a whisper, "Tell me this is not her?" as I pointed to the picture of the baby crying.

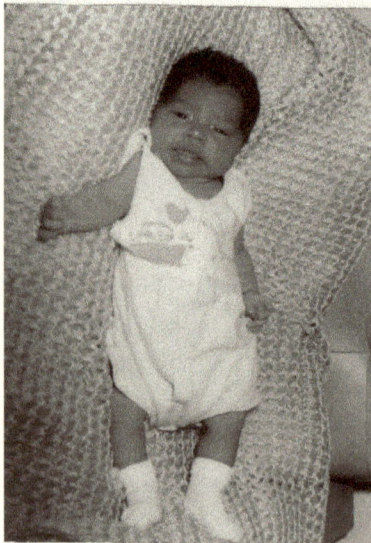

Marisa Crying

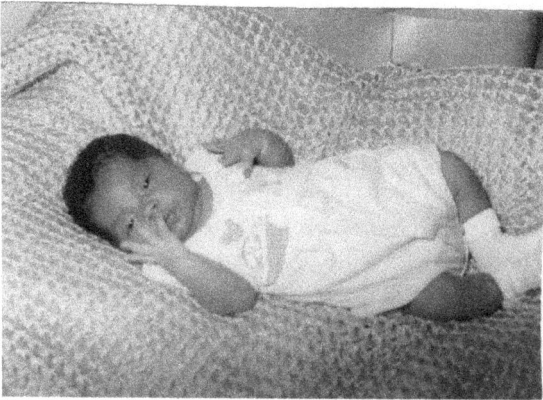

*Angel sent me two pictures. One showed
Marisa crying. The picture facing me was the
one where she was crying.*

What I didn't know then that I know now is,
when Marisa cries, she looks pretty damn awful.
Her eyes look like somebody punched her out
and her lips become red and swollen, as well. Her
lips, which are quite full and beautiful, swell up
incredibly. Well, that was the first picture I saw
of her, not very complimentary at all. Although,
she was a beautiful baby, those were just plain
bad pictures. Edwin was so mad at me that day.
I spoiled the day for him and he didn't speak to
me for several nights. So much for a special
moment and my fantasy! Then, I remembered
what the woman from LAPA had said about the
babies not having any resemblance to us. Well,
she sure didn't! She looked so different. I didn't

know how to feel. I was scared. Thank the Lord that Angel took two pictures and sent me one where she was calm. Still, not a great picture either. I then took a breath.

During the next four months, I carried my little girl's pictures with me, even the one where she was crying, and I looked at them every day memorizing every feature of her face. But I couldn't bond with pictures no matter how many times I looked at them. I had to admit, I was nervous about being able to love a child that looked so unlike us; so, unlike me. Could I love her? Did pregnant women feel this way about the baby in their bellies? Were these normal feelings? I was just so scared of my own insecurities. I felt guilty to even dare have these feelings. After everything we had been through and we were now about to be parents. I didn't know what to think. I was driving myself nuts with these thoughts. I was afraid to share my feelings with Edwin, but he knew me well. One night he asked me how I felt about the baby. I didn't answer him. I answered him with a question. Women are good at that... answering a question with a question, especially me. I am pro at it. I asked him how he felt. He then said, "Babe, I can't wait to see her and hold her in my arms." He was so excited about finally being a daddy. His face just lit up when he talked about the baby. I was so surprised, since he never shared his feelings like that before. I gave him a big hug with tears in my eyes. His enthusiasm helped me get a grip on my feelings. So, I stopped worrying about how the baby looked and concentrated on getting ready for her to come home.

February finally came, and the lawyer submitted our petition for adoption. It was going to take a while. He wanted me to be prepared. February passed with no problem. Angel assured me that it could be late March. But March came and still no word as to when to come down. In the meantime, I called every week to talk to Elvira and Angel and hear the baby through the phone. I could hear her cooing and Elvira's daughter would try to make her laugh and I could hear the baby through the phone. These phone calls were packed with emotion and I could picture my little girl on the other end sitting on Elvira's lap while Necky tickled her and made the baby giggle. She sounded so cute and happy.

In late March, I was invited to go over to my girlfriend Esther's house for dinner to celebrate her father's birthday. I was watching *Jaws* on TV and in no hurry to get going. Suddenly Edwin yelled at me. I was so engrossed in watching the movie. I had one leg inside one side of my pants and the other sticking out of it. "Honey, hurry up!" I jumped, and he walked over and turned off the TV. I felt like a little girl being scolded. He smiled at me as I finished getting dressed.

When I arrived at Esther's house, everyone shouted, "Surprise!" I looked behind me to see if her father was standing behind us. I still didn't catch on that she, Edwin, and my parents had gotten together to give me a baby shower. Everyone was there! My entire family and close friends, including Susan and her husband, Persio and Blanca, and Izzy and his family. Then I saw all the baby things and I started to cry. So did everyone else.

On one side of the living room was a huge table filled with gifts and a special chair with balloons and more gifts all around the chair. I was in no hurry to open them. I just wanted to remember this wonderful day, taking in all the details. After we had dinner, it was time to open the gifts. Each gift was wrapped with so much care and I could see that everyone really went out of their way to make this day memorable. I didn't really want to open them. But of course, I did. It was so nice to open everything. In the end.... surrounded by so many beautiful baby clothes......my innermost thoughts were, when will I see my little girl in these clothes and see her little hands hold these cute baby toys. I was so overwhelmed with emotion that day. I never thought I would have a baby shower. I didn't even think that my family would be planning one for me. I was truly touched by everyone's kindness.

Chapter 8:

Falling in Love

In the first week of April, we finally got "the call" from Angel at 8:00 p.m.! We had a court date set for April 22nd. Oh my God, I was so excited. Angel instructed us to arrive several days in advance, but there was one more hurdle to pass. He indicated that I had to phone him the day before we were scheduled to fly out because anything could change at the last minute. I don't really know how I lived through those awful weeks leading up to the day we were supposed to travel to Paraguay. I tried to keep busy at work and at home. I couldn't sleep. I couldn't eat. I couldn't rest. I was tied up in knots inside. Plus,

Edwin was driving me crazy worrying about how much time we needed to spend in Paraguay because he was the lead candidate for an assistant principalship. I told him I didn't really know. We had to have an open ticket for the return flight. This bothered him and me too, but I was less worried. I knew what had to be done at the US Consulate's Office once we had the adoption decree, but the rest was a little unclear to me. All I knew was that my little girl was coming home with us and I left the rest in God's hands.

When I put in for my leave of absence, I requested that all my accrued vacation be paid in advance. I had miscalculated, and I was handed a check of over $1,000. In addition, my parents also handed me another $1,000 for expenses in Paraguay. I was so grateful I received the money we needed for our trip. I was surprised and relieved.

Friday, April 15, 1988 finally came, the day before we were to fly out. Our luggage was packed, but I refused to pack for the baby. I couldn't bring myself to put her baby clothes in the luggage. I just couldn't do it until I knew for sure I was flying out. At 8:00 p.m., I placed the called to Angel. I nervously asked him if everything was all right for us to fly out the next day and I held my breath and closed my eyes. He said all was in order with the court. I started to cry again. I guess he didn't realize how much strain I was under coming so close, just to be told there was more waiting. I gave him our flight schedule. We were leaving New York on Saturday, April 16, 1988, flying to Miami at 6 p.m. and catching the midnight flight from Miami on LAP Airlines to Paraguay, arriving Sunday morning at 8:30 a.m. on April 17, 1988. After I hung up the phone, I ran to the baby's room and started crying again, as I packed her things. What a joy it will be to finally be able to see the baby in all those clothes at last, I thought. I remember I stayed in the baby's room for a long time sitting in the rocking chair looking at the beautiful lavender room Edwin and I created and thanking God for his kindness over me, over us, over the baby. A baby, picked by God himself. Our lives were about to change. It felt simply awesome!

The next day, my girlfriend, Esther, came up to our apartment to get us. She and her husband were taking us to the airport. Our parents were coming also to the airport. Esther found me in the baby's room placing some additional clothing in the baby's luggage. "Hi mommy, you are ready to go?" I turned around with tears in my eyes again. "I can't believe this day is finally here Es. How many times have we talked about this day and it is here. I am so happy, I wish I could just freeze this moment." She was crying too.

"I know how hard the waiting time has been. But it's finally here. You must promise to call me when you have the baby in your arms and remember that I love you and you are going to be just fine. You know I am going to be counting down the days to when you come home with my Goddaughter." Es was like a sister to me. We were both born on the same day, but she was older than me by five years. She would always tell me on our birthday, "Girl, you are catching up to me." We would always laugh. "Okay C, focus! You have everything?" Es always called me "C" - short for Clari. "Yes, I have everything, I just remembered that it will be cool in New York when we arrive, and I just put another outfit that was a little warmer in my luggage. It was so hard to pack for the baby, not really knowing her actual weight. I kept asking Elvira if the clothes I sent fit or were they big. She would just say everything fits. So, I didn't know what to take."

"C, it will be fine. You are not going to a place that doesn't have stores. If it doesn't fit, you just buy what you need. That is the least of it." Of course. I was so glad she was there with me. I needed her support so much. "You are right. I am not going to Siberia." We both laughed as she helped me close the baby's luggage.

Everyone stayed with us at the airport until it was time to go through security. They videotaped us and asked us to say a few words. That was really nice of them. I had a book to read for the plane ride. Like I was really going to read. Not! It was close to the time to say goodbye. This was going to be hard on my parents. My father held me for a long time. I felt him shaking. Then I let go and told him, "Dad, don't worry, and have faith I am coming home with your granddaughter. Everything is going to be fine. I will call as soon as we arrive at Angel's home." I hugged my mother, who was crying too. I hugged Edwin's parents and asked them to please keep in touch with my parents during this time. I then said my goodbyes to Es. "Remember "C" everything is going to be OK. I will call mom and dad often when you are away." My parent's adopted Es as their other daughter, and she called them mom and dad too and they grew to love her. Suddenly, we were on our way.

The plane ride to Miami was pleasant. We walked all around the airport, looked into the various shops and finally sat down to wait until midnight. I thought midnight would never come. The plan took off on time and I tried to read my book. I really couldn't though. I kept looking outside. It felt like the plane was in outer space, we were so far above the clouds and I could see thunder and lightning below the clouds, it was a little frightening. So, I didn't look again. I walked around the plane a little to stretch my legs. Everyone looked a little foreign to me. I could hear people speaking in another language that I didn't understand. I figured it was Portuguese.

We finally arrived in Asuncion at exactly 8:30 a.m. As we were collecting the luggage at the airport in Paraguay, I glanced up and saw a couple holding a baby standing behind the glass doors separating the arriving passengers from the waiting families. I knew that it was Angel and Elvira. They waved at us, recognizing us as we walked towards them. We had sent pictures of us and they reciprocated with sending pictures of their family.

My heart wanted to come out of my chest, it was beating so fast. My hands were shaking. When we finally got to them, I hugged them both and hugged their two children Necky and Danny, but I wouldn't look at my baby girl in Elvira's arms. I was still nervous. I could hear Angel greeting Edwin behind me. I couldn't believe my reaction. Finally, Elvira said to me in Spanish, "No quieres a su hija?" "Don't you want your daughter?" I looked at Elvira as she placed the baby in my arms. I still refused to look at her. I closed my eyes as I held her high above me. Everyone was quiet as I did this, watching for my reaction. I took a breath and opened my eyes to look at my little girl for the first time. She gave me this big squeal and dribbled all over my face and started to giggle, and I just hugged her to me. Everyone started to clap. With tears flowing down my face, I looked at her again and covered her face with kisses, until Edwin snatched her from my arms. I was in love for the second time in my life! We were both crying as we held our baby girl. We couldn't take our eyes off her. We were in awe of her beauty. Elvira and Angel watched us with big smiles on their faces.

The car they had was small and we were packed in with their kids sitting on either side of us. The baby was sitting on my lap and we both couldn't stop looking at her. The baby dribbled all over my face and hands and I loved it. I felt like it was holy water from heaven. When we arrived at Angel's home, Elvira had prepared a light lunch. They set aside the upstairs bedroom for us, which had its own bathroom. The bedroom had a full-size bed and a small twin bed for the baby. Angel explained that the baby was a good sleeper and didn't move around much. He instructed me to put a pillow on each side of her and that she would be fine. He also had a mosquito net around the twin bed.

I asked if we could call our parents and he said, "Of course." I told him that we would reimburse him for all the calls we made to New York. We decided to just make one phone call for now and let my mom call everyone in the family. The phone only rang twice. She was anxiously waiting to hear from us. "Mom, I am in Angel's home and I am holding the baby." I could hear mom crying and barely able to talk. She gave the phone to my dad. "Clari," he said, really relieved to hear me." "Hi Dad, I have your granddaughter in my arms and she is beautiful." "I can't wait to see her," he said to me in Spanish. I let him speak to Angel to put him at ease that we were safe.

After lunch, we went upstairs to relax as it was Siesta time. The baby was exhausted, and she had pooped and needed a bath. When I opened her diaper, surprise! I found green poop and a green/blue bottom for added color coordination.... something not to forget to tell her about one day. Actually, I had read about these spots. And LAPA also told us about them and for parents not to think their baby was abused in any way when they saw these spots. The green/blue spots on her bottom are called Mongolian blue spots, which are common among darker skinned infants, such as those who are of Indian descent in Latin America.

The baby was fussing because I was a stranger, and I am sure she was missing Elvira. Elvira told me to give her a bath as it would calm her down. This was another first for me. Elvira helped me through the bath. It was difficult to do, because in Elvira's home, there was no tub, only a shower. I had to get in the shower with the baby while I was holding her with the shower coming down on both of us. But she loved the bath and giggled through the whole process. I handed the baby over to Elvira while I dried myself off and took out some of the clothes I brought for the baby. Elvira then left us. I was all thumbs as I tried to put on her diaper and went through two diapers sealing the diapers along with my thumbs in the process and ripping the diaper to get my thumbs out. Edwin was laughing at me. "Look at me Edwin, I am so nervous that I can't even put on a simple diaper." But, third time was the charm and I got it right. I took my time putting on the powder and lotion and by the time I finished dressing the baby, she was fast asleep. I was exhausted too and I laid her down between me and Edwin and we all napped together. Angel looked in on us and was amazed that the baby was asleep. He said she fussed a lot during siesta time. Then he said the nicest thing to me. "I think she was waiting for you, too. She is with her mommy now." I was a mommy now. I felt fulfilled.

Elvira saved all her medical documents when she was first taken to the Pediatrician and every month thereafter. On Friday, April 22, 1988, we had our court appointment, and Angel told me he knew the judge personally. It was such a long wait. We were in court all morning. Then, we had to go to some other offices where we had to get fingerprinted and get an identity card. We didn't get back to Elvira's until the evening. She was anxiously waiting for us. The baby was hysterically crying, very tired and hungry. I had run out of milk and only had water to give her. Elvira knew and had a warm bottle of milk ready and waiting. The baby drank it so fast that she got the hiccups right after. We both laughed and then she looked at us and fell right to sleep. I knew exactly how she felt.

We stayed with Angel and Elvira for three precious weeks. We went to the US Consulate's office that same week when we received the adoption decree to petition for the baby's Visa. The staff at the Consulate's office were very nice to us and helped us through all the steps we had to take to get the Visa. And Angel helped us through all the remaining legal paperwork. By the end of two weeks, we had accomplished a great deal. On the weekends, Angel took us sightseeing and it was very nice traveling with them and their children, and of course our little girl. We took lots of pictures. She got to know us and got used to us taking her for long walks during siesta time. We couldn't nap during siesta time and it was so quiet around Angel's neighborhood. Edwin and I took turns holding Marisa. Sometimes, when Edwin held her, I would make funny faces and Marisa would giggle and laugh out loud. She was really loud. I loved it and we would both laugh with the baby.

Elvira and Angel lived in a residential area of Asuncion. The homes looked very much like the homes in Puerto Rico. So, it didn't look so foreign to us. We found a local grocery store where we bought snacks for Elvira's children. They always looked forward to them when they arrived after school. Angel told me I was spoiling them. I asked him to let me because it gave me pleasure to see them excited when they got home. After school, Danny and Necky always played with the baby when they first came home and ate their snacks. Then an hour later, it was time to do their homework before dinner time.

We had already spent two weeks with them in their home and I knew Elvira and Angel were going to miss the baby. They purposely separated themselves from the baby during this time to lessen the pain when we left. We decided to ask them to baptize her, being that they were Catholic and more importantly, loved Marisa so much. They were secretly hoping that we would ask, but didn't dare approach us because they felt we would have her baptized in New York. But they were truly touched by our request, most especially Elvira. On April 30, 1988, Angel and Elvira became Marisa's Godparents, which meant that they would have a special bond with her during her growing up years, even from a distance. This meant a lot to Elvira and to me. I missed not having my family around for this special ceremony. However, I felt it was the right thing to do. During this brief stay in their home, we became a family. And like a family, you share good times and sad times.

When the day came that we had to leave, it was a happy moment for us and a very sad moment for Elvira and Angel. Elvira confided that she and Angel wanted to adopt the baby as well, but realized how long we had waited and couldn't do it. She said that she and Angel were giving us a gift, since they already had two children and they just couldn't be so selfish, although they were going to miss Marisa immensely. Elvira and I cried together. I couldn't even imagine how she could give the baby up after four months. I was only with her for three weeks and I couldn't be away from her for a minute. Elvira told me that her children would help her through it. Necky and Danny were always around us and we adored having them with us. They played with the baby and I could tell that they loved her a great deal, too. At the airport, we all hugged each other, and it was hard for them to let us go. Then, Edwin broke down and was crying too. It was a lot a pressure for him also. Angel gave him a big hug. As we went through security, I didn't want to look back, but I did, and I saw Elvira crying on Angel's shoulders. I started to cry, too.

Chapter 9:

Fulfillment

When I boarded the plane in Paraguay to go home, I started to really weep in earnest. I was finally bringing home my baby girl to join our family. When the plane set down in Miami, I was happy to be in the United States. What a coincidence that we flew from Paraguay the day before Mother's Day, to arrive in New York on Mother's Day, May 8, 1988. Marisa was exactly five months old. We had to stay overnight in Miami and catch an early morning flight to New York. I called my mom when we got to the hotel. She and dad were anxiously waiting by the phone for my call.

"Hi Mom, I have your Mother's Day gift in my arms." I could hear her crying on the other end. I could hear my dad screaming in the background with happiness. When mom spoke, she told me that Dad almost had a nervous breakdown when I left for Paraguay. She didn't keep me long on the phone, Marisa was starting to fuss, and I was so very tired, and my back was killing me.

We arrived in New York at 10:30 a.m. the next morning, May 8, 1988. Our entire family and many of our friends, including Izzy and his family, Susan and her family, and Persio and his family, were at the airport. My mother was the first to greet us and we were both crying as she hugged me with Marisa in my arms together. Everyone surrounded us, taking turns with the baby and asking us questions. My mom took Marisa from my arms and started speaking to her in Spanish and crying at the same time. We stayed at the airport for two hours, when Marisa finally let out a loud cry! It was time to go home! When I finally got home with Marisa, I broke down and cried when I put her in her crib that was empty for so many months. My baby girl was finally home! I felt truly blessed and grateful.

In the following chapter are photos of this special journey.

Chapter 10:

Special Thanks

People have told me that I am a special person for adopting a child. I don't feel special; I feel fulfilled, blessed, and immensely grateful. If a miracle ever had to be documented, I think the series of events that led me to my little girl qualifies. She was so beautiful and perfect in every way. To think that Angel and Elvira agreed to take care of her until all the documentation was ready for us to appear before a Judge in Paraguay was so giving and wonderful. Elvira took a leave of absence for two and a half months to take care of her, which was a really huge sacrifice. Marisa received a lot of love from these two special people and their two children, Necky and Danny. I felt honored by and grateful for the gift they gave to me; to us. I can't help but feel humbled once again before God for this precious gift because, that is how I see my little girl, a gift chosen by God.

I am also grateful that nothing happened to me or my documents when I had to leave them in the Consulate's Office at the World Trade Center back in 1987. Who was to know that in fourteen years, we would lose the World Trade Centers, along with so many people on 9/11. So much was lost on that day. On that horrible day, I thought about the families who might have had their documents there waiting for the Consulate to sign, all lost, and then the long wait for the Consulate to open a new office in a different location.

Marisa took her first footsteps in front of her grandmother (my mother-in-law) who passed away when Marisa was about a year and half. Her grandfather (my father-in-law) lived with us for many years. He passed away when Marisa was about eleven years old. Marisa was dearly loved by her other grandfather, my dad, who I believe reminded her a lot of Angel. She used to go crazy when she saw him and would cry uncontrollably when we removed her from his arms, when it was time to go home. My mother used to get jealous that she didn't get the same reaction. Today, Marisa has a close bond with my mother, who is still living. I remember that my mother spent all day with Marisa on her first day at home, playing with her, feeding her, and changing her while I caught up on much needed rest.

I fondly recall that on the baby's first Christmas, my family went nuts forgetting we lived in an apartment and nearly bought out Toys R Us. I am exaggerating, of course. But they did try to buy every toy in the place. I was touched.

Marisa's Godfather, Angel, traveled from Paraguay to visit with us and spend time with Marisa when she was about four years old. Unfortunately, Elvira was not able to travel. I will be forever grateful to her Godparents who provided love and affection in the first few precious months and made the ultimate sacrifice for two people that were strangers but who, in the end, became family. I want to especially thank the angel sent by God, our cousin, Izzy. God chose well, as Izzy was Pastor of a church in Boca Raton, Florida for many years. If it wasn't for him, Marisa would not have been part of my life. And lastly, I want thank Edwin and our family, who lifted me up and supported me through this incredible experience. This was truly a special journey.

A child is a gift from God. Treasure it always.

Baby Marisa sleeping in our bedroom in Paraguay.

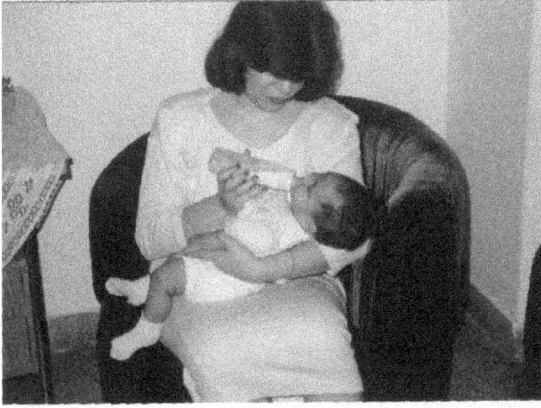

Feeding Marisa on the day we were going to court

Marisa being baptized in Paraguay by her Godparents, who took care of her for her first four months. Here she is wearing the outfit I purchased at the World Trade Center.

Sightseeing in Paraguay

More Sightseeing in Paraguay

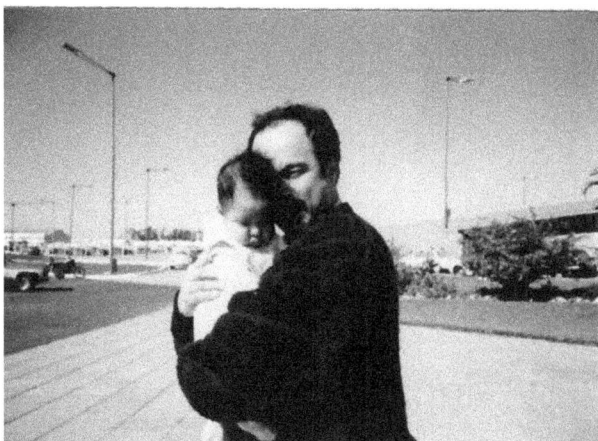

*First time we saw Marisa
at the airport in Paraguay*

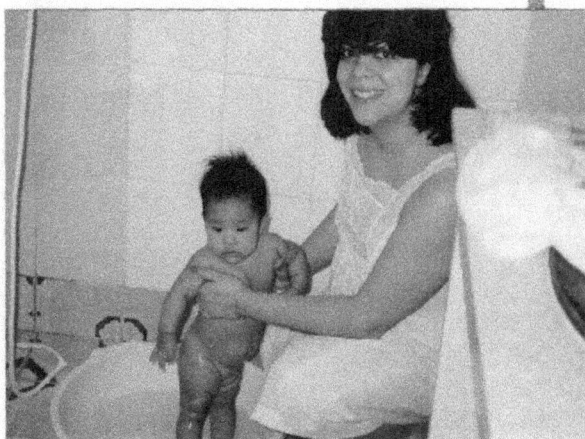

First Bath with Marisa. We roughed it a bit.

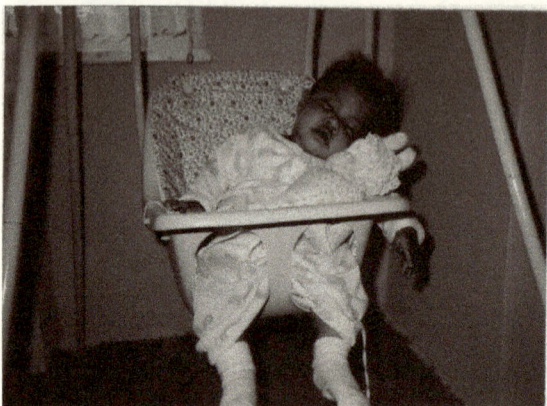

Marisa home at last!

Pre-k Graduation. Look at those dimples!

Marisa

Clari Diaz

Chapter 11:

William

January 1990

My husband approached me about starting the adoption process for an infant boy. I was quite happy with my little girl. I reminded him that he didn't keep his promise to be around, now that he was a father. He kept working and expanding his business. As a result, I was alone again. I certainly wasn't sad and I didn't feel alone. I had my little girl to keep me busy. I took her everywhere with me. She was such a good baby and loved being outside. I was so happy.

My husband explained that I had my little girl and saw my fulfillment as a mother, and he wanted to feel the same. Hence, he wanted a son. The thought of going through another adoption was overwhelming. All the paperwork would fall on my shoulders, once again. It was an exhausting process, coupled with suffering the inevitable the setbacks. I knew from experience that the process would take its toll on my emotions.

In his defense, I do recall that I originally wanted to have two children and I wanted them to be two years apart. I grew up as an only child and it was a lonely and sheltered existence for me. I did grow up in a family-oriented home that was warm and loving, but it was lonely, nevertheless. I didn't want that for my little girl.

When Marisa turned two years old in January of 1990, I contacted the lawyer I met at the US Consulate in Asuncion called Agustin. I selected him because he took care of everything from the court appearance, right through to dealing with the US Consulate's Office for the baby's Visa. The lawyer we had for Marisa only helped us up to the court appearance. Marisa's Godfather, Angel, helped us through the rest, since he was a judge and lawyer. I contacted Agustin via phone. I was pleasantly surprised that he remembered me as I had let him know, while I was in Paraguay, that I would be contacting him in two years for a second adoption. I even left my contact information with him. Sadly, Agustin let me know that, due to a change in the Presidency in Paraguay, all adoptions were closed until further notice. However, he advised that I start collecting the various documents needed for the adoption. So, we went through them.

1. The Home Study
2. The Family History
3. Two Letters of Reference
4. Psychological Report
5. Medical Report
6. Letters of Employment Verification, including salary and date of hire
7. Latest IRS Tax Return
8. Certificate of Good Conduct

He reminded me that all the documents had to be notarized, authenticated, and translated by a licensed translator and stamped by the Paraguayan Consulate. He indicated that approval from the Consulate should wait until he lets me know that I can submit the documents to him.

I asked if there was anything else and Agustin informed me, not at this time. Regarding his fee, he said let's leave that until we start the process. I told him that I was interested in adopting a baby boy this time, since I already had my little girl. I was overwhelmed with starting this process all over again. I decided not to think about it too much and just start the process. I did have time on my side, so that was a relief.

I decided not to contact Angel, Marisa's Godfather, about the second adoption, because as much as I wanted to take Marisa with me, her grandparents were not in agreement. They offered to take care of her while I was adopting in Paraguay. I wanted to visit with her Godparents, but they refused to listen to me. It was going to be too hard on my parents to be without their granddaughter. They were so attached to her. At the same time, it was a great time for her Godparents to have quality time with her. I was in a quandary and I also was a bit apprehensive about bringing her with me. I felt guilty about the possibility of not taking Marisa with us to Paraguay. There was a limit to what I can deal with all at once. So, I put these thoughts on the back burner for the time being, so to speak.

After I completed my call with Agustin, I decided to look over the list of all the documents required. I just needed to upgrade the home study to include the adoption of Marisa. We both still worked in the same establishments, the salaries were different so new tax forms were required. That would be the last document to obtain, which would be determined by when the adoptions would open once again in Paraguay. I contacted the person who did Spanish translations to make sure she was still doing this type of work. We needed a psychology report. Maybe that was a good place to start. So, I looked up the list of Psychologists and started to make calls to make the first appointment. The thought of doing this all over again was truly overwhelming, especially having gone through an international adoption and knowing the emotions we were going to go through once again. It was 1990 when I started to gather the documents for my baby boy adoption.

June 1988

A year before, in the summer of 1988, I decided to try IVF (In-Vitro Fertilization) once again. Since I already had Marisa, maybe this time around I would be less stressed about going through the procedure. I was pleasantly surprised that I didn't need to hold my water when it was time to remove the eggs because sonogram technology had advanced to initiating the scan intravaginally. Wow! I was happy about that. Also, the drugs were different, but my butt would still hurt. No getting around that.

One day as I was visiting with Edwin's mother, she sat me down and requested that I name my son William, regardless if I gave birth to a boy or adopted one. I didn't quite understand this request because she already had a grandson named William, who they called Billy. The reason for the request was, she had a son named William that died at the age of fifteen, before the birth of my husband, Edwin. In fact, when William died, she was not aware that she was pregnant with Edwin.

That evening I argued with Edwin because I didn't want to name my son "William." Edwin asked me why we were arguing about this, especially since I was indeed not pregnant, and I had not started the process for the second adoption. I told him, I just wanted him to know how I felt about his mother's request. He told me to just drop it.

It really was not that simple. His mother was diagnosed with breast cancer and the cancer had metastasized to her bones. She was doing well with her Chemo and Radiation, but the prognosis was not good. So, part of me couldn't just drop this request so easily. Maybe it could be a middle name, I thought. My mother-in-law loved Marisa very much and although she was not doing well, on her good days, I let the baby stay with her. In fact, much to her pleasure, Marisa took her first steps in front of her loving grandmother at fourteen months. She really cherished that moment. And I was truly happy for her.

As all this was going on in my life, I tried IVF again and endured the injections and visits to the infertility clinic. Marisa was about sixteen months old by then and a very active little girl.

She was a doll. I could take her anywhere. She loved to go out and be the center of attention.

I produced thirteen eggs once again and Edwin fertilized five. I decided to take them all. Maybe I would be lucky if all the embryos were together and perhaps thrived. But I had my doubts, once again, that it would happen. I wasn't being negative. It was just intuition. And I could sense it. I simply couldn't help these feelings when they came.

In the end, the results were indeed negative. When Marisa turned two, I decided to contact the lawyer, Agustin, to start the adoption process for a baby boy. Sadly, in the spring of 1989, Edwin's mother passed away from her fight with cancer. She died young, in her early 70s. Marisa's presence helped the entire family during this sad time in our lives, most especially with Edwin and his father, Marisa's other grandfather. He adored Marisa.

January 1992

Three years later, in January of 1992, Agustin called to let me know that the adoptions were opening once again. He asked me if I had any documents to give him. To his surprise, I let him know that I was ready with all the documents, except for my taxes from the previous year, which were in the process of being submitted. He instructed me to send him whatever I had so he could start the process in Paraguay and to send along a copy of our tax return documents when they were ready, for which I complied.

Once again, I had to go to the World Trade Center to leave the documents and return in four days to retrieve them. Once again, I felt that I left my life in their hands. I again shopped in the basement and picked out an outfit for the baby. As I left the building, I once again looked back as I did when I was in the process of adopting Marisa and assuring myself that nothing could ever happen at the World Trade Centers. As we know, tragedy did strike eight years later.

June 1992

In June of 1992, Agustin called to let me know he was sending a picture of a baby boy. I was excited. When I received the picture, I looked at it. I showed it to Edwin. I didn't feel anything when I looked at the baby's picture. Oddly, I put the picture back in the envelope in which it came and placed it in my draw with my adoption documents. In August of 1992, Agustin called and sadly let me know that the birth mother changed her mind. However, he was quick to inform me that there was another picture coming of a new baby boy. So, before I could react, I said okay and waited anxiously once again.

When the picture arrived, Edwin and I looked at the picture and we both had the same reaction. Well, I really don't recall how he felt about the new picture, but I felt nothing. Oddly, once again, I placed the picture back in the envelope and filed it with the adoption documents. I felt funny when I did this, but I did it just the same. I didn't really want to think anything. But, the premonition that I would not adopt this baby either, was there. I recall, I was just protecting myself from more disappointment without realizing it.

October 1992

In October of 1992, Agustin called! As soon as I heard his voice, however, I knew something terrible had happened. His voice said it all, before the awful words he uttered next, nearly killed me.... the baby was very sick. He had to be hospitalized, given how ill he was. The clinical staff couldn't save him, and he died of a severe stomach virus. I was totally devastated when he finished relating the events that led up to the baby's death. The sadness in his voice was overwhelming. I asked him why he didn't let me know, I could have gone down to provide some comfort to the baby. I was actively crying now on the phone. He explained gently that I was not legally the baby's mother and I would not have been permitted to give care to the baby. I asked if he was well cared for by the staff at the hospital. I was crying and upset. He assured me that they did all they could for the baby. Then, I received a double stab in the heart when, sadly, he told me that he didn't have another baby boy and asked me if I was still interested in pursuing the adoption. Through my tears, I told him yes, I was still interested and to please let me know when a baby boy became available. I hung up. Edwin was not home yet, so he didn't know about these very sad developments.

When he arrived, he found me in the bedroom crying my eyes out. I told him what happened. I let him know that I didn't want anyone in the family to know. If they should ask, we can tell them we are waiting, nothing further. I simply didn't want to talk about this sad news. I said a prayer that night for the baby. I couldn't get the picture of this little baby fighting for his life all alone in the hospital with no mother by his side to give him comfort. The pain I felt in my heart was unbearable. And I just couldn't deal with the pain and sadness with my family. It would be too much for me. It was easier to just let me grieve for the baby on my own.

December 1992

It was two days before New Year's Eve when our lives changed as parents and I understood that everything we experienced was spiritual, amazing, and divine. On that day in December, I thought to myself, boy I could use some good news before the New Year. As soon as I thought it, the phone rang and something inside me told me it was Agustin! As a result, I answered the phone with excitement in my voice. And it was Agustin! I scare myself sometimes, truly. His voice sounded so excited on the phone. He announced, "Senora Clari, I've been trying to reach you for two days." I told him we were away for a few days and had just returned. He then said, "A new baby boy is available, and nothing is going to go wrong with this adoption." He let me know that he interviewed the birth mother very well and the baby was born healthy and he assured me that all was going to go smooth. Then he said the best news, "Senora Clari, I just mailed the picture with all his birth information to you." I responded, with tears rolling down, "Thank you, Agustin. That's the best New Year's news ever!"

I suddenly became so very excited. I could hear him laughing at my response. He reminded me that the courts would be closed for the next two months and that he would proceed with filing the adoption papers as soon as they opened, and he would be in touch in the early spring.

January 1993

For the next two weeks, I anxiously waited for my baby boy's picture. Since Edwin got home first, I would call every day, "Anything yet, babe?" He would always respond, "Don't you think I would have called you by now?" "I know, I know," I would respond. "Just anxious, babe." He knew I was.

I finally got the picture after the second week of January on a Saturday. I remembered that when I got the envelope, I tore it open right on the front steps of my home. It was freezing outside, but I didn't care. I couldn't wait to see him! I remember that I didn't feel this way about the other pictures. Amazing! When I glanced at the picture, I gasped, "Oh my God, this is my son!" I took the picture and put it in a frame and placed it in the living room for everyone to see. I was so excited! When Edwin got home, I told him we got the picture of our new son! He looked at it too and hugged me. "Yes, this is him," he said too! Wow!

I started to call everyone in my family, to let them know that our son's picture had arrived, and I couldn't wait to show him off. The last person I contacted was Edwin's sister, Iris. She asked me the details of his birth; how many pounds he weighed. I told her the baby weighed eight pounds and then she asked if I had his birth date. I told her, "Oh yes, he was born on December 17th."

Iris then gasped, "Oh my God Clari, that is my late brother's birthday, the one who died at fifteen years of age." I was simply stunned! I remembered her late mother's request, which only Edwin knew about, but not anyone else in the family. She surprisingly said to me, "I guess you are going to name him William." I then told Iris about the conversation Aida, her late mother, had with me almost three years ago when Marisa was only six months old. As I told her, I was experiencing goose bumps on my arms. I told her that I definitely was going to name my son "William." I felt that my mother-in-law's spirit came through to us and became part of this happy moment in our lives. It simply was fate, faith, and love.

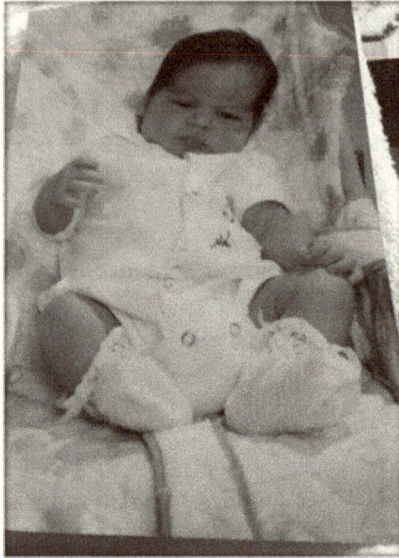

William – 8 Lbs.

March – April 1993

The courts opened in March and our adoption papers were filed with the Paraguayan Court. In early April, Agustin called to let us know that our court date was on April 22nd. This was too much! I couldn't believe it was five years to the day of Marisa's adoption! The coincidence was overwhelming. This really was divine intervention at work. I was so grateful because I knew that God had His hand in this. I started calling my family, but no one was around to learn that I was in "ADOPTION LABOR!" Oh, my goodness, I was so excited!

The date to leave was finally upon us, but the only huge difference was leaving Marisa behind. She was now five years old and in pre-kindergarten. Her teachers all knew about the adoption and I told them this was going to be difficult for her being without her mommy and daddy. We prepared her, of course, and let her know that we were bringing her baby brother home to join our family. She was happy about being a big sister, but confused about not being able to go with us.

The day finally came. My parents took us to the airport, but when we arrived, they had decided not to go into the airport with us. I started to cry because I thought, at a minimum, I had at least another hour with my little girl! But my father explained that it would be too frightening for Marisa to see us go through a security gate and then watch us disappear. Getting out of the car would be less dramatic for her. He was right of course, but I was not prepared as they didn't discuss these arrangements with me. I started to cry, and Marisa started to cry too, holding me as I put so many kisses on her little face. I left her screaming in the car. I was totally devastated and unprepared for the emotions that ensued as a result and the drama that was about to come. I suddenly felt such sadness and my heart felt heavy in my chest.

Consequently, when I got inside the airport, I had a total melt down in the middle of the airport. I became hysterical. I started crying, "How could I leave my baby girl? I CAN'T DO THIS! I CAN'T DO THIS!" I screamed to Edwin. Then I said, "I want to CANCEL the trip!" I didn't want to go through with the adoption! People started gathering. Edwin was beside himself. He didn't know what to do either. He just reacted as best he could. By this time, I was not crying. I was weeping hysterically. Edwin's leadership skills kicked in at this moment and he used all his love and powers of persuasion to calm me down. He grabbed me by the shoulders and looked at me. He shook me and said, "Clari, you are so strong *you can do anything*. And YOU can do this. WE can DO THIS! Just think babe, in a few hours, you will have beautiful William in your arms! Marisa is with her grandparents. She is in the best care. We will call her when we get to Paraguay and you will see she will be fine." He looked at me again. I shook my head up and down for a sign of yes. People started clapping and patting me and Edwin on the back, wishing us luck. I then marched into the bathroom to clean my face and pull myself together. But I just cried some more and let it all out until I couldn't cry any more. As I came out, of the "Ladies' Room," I showed some determination. "Some" is the key word here. But I was hurting badly inside.

Unbeknown to me, I was going to be very busy with little William. The route to Paraguay was a bit different. We had a layover in Sao Paulo, Brazil, but we were literally running from one gate to another. As a result, when we arrived in Asuncion at 9:30 a.m., our luggage was not on the plane. We were told that the luggage would be on the next flight from Sao Paulo. We had to wait almost two hours for our luggage.

When we arrived, we were met by Agustin, and sadly, he didn't have our baby with him. I was really upset about this, especially after the emotional turmoil at the JFK Airport. He informed us that the baby was in the hospital for a week with a stomach virus. He didn't want to tell us because he didn't want me to panic due to what happened with the previous baby. He told me that William was fine and out of the hospital. Then he gave us strict instructions.

"Listen to me carefully. What I want you to do when you get to the hotel is have the staff install a crib in your room. Unpack all the baby clothes and your clothes. The hotel staff is aware that you are adopting a baby and will help you get everything ready for him. Remember that since the baby has been sick, he will need a lot of care and you both will need to rest. I want you both to get at least two hours sleep in the hotel. I am bringing the baby over at 6:00 p.m. tonight."

It was 12:30 p.m. when we arrived at the hotel. He also let us know that there were other

American couples staying at the hotel who were also adopting.

When we arrived at the hotel, the staff immediately went to work and got us situated in our room, immediately getting us the crib. All the adopting couples were on the same floor. This helped the hotel staff take care of our needs. We were assigned a maid who was instructed to help us get anything we needed for the baby, including hot water for formula and food for us in the room, if we didn't want to go to the restaurant to eat. I remember, we loved the #10 chicken sandwich, which we ordered that afternoon to go with some juice and water.

The room had two double beds, coupled with enough space for a crib and a nice large bathroom. We told them we wanted to make a call to New York, and we did so immediately. My parents told me Marisa was fine. A little sad we weren't with her, but she knew that we would come home with her baby brother. She of course had no concept of time and the pre-K teachers would help her with that. I told them I would alert them with a date when we were coming home. We had no appointments the next day. Agustin wanted us to take time to get to know the baby.

I forced myself to sleep for two hours. We were both tired from the trip, so we did sleep after I had unpacked everything. At 5:30 p.m., I opened our hotel door to wait for Agustin to come with the baby. I was very anxious.

All of the sudden, there he was. Agustin was holding this little, tiny baby that certainly didn't look like he was four months old. He looked much younger. He looked simply terrified, a bit gaunt and gray. He didn't cry at all when Agustin put him in my arms. He just looked scared. Poor baby. This was so different from Marisa who was a happy baby having had the love of her Godparents. William was in an orphanage for four months and there was no way around this. It was how government managed the orphaned babies.

Agustin gave me the baby's feeding schedule and I noticed that William was being given starch, juice and vegetables and very little formula. No wonder he had a stomach virus. I inquired why he had this feeding schedule. I explained that in America, babies are started on food at about five months, and just cereal for the first month. He explained that in Paraguay, the babies are started on food at two months. I was shocked!

Since he had a virus, I assumed the baby must have diarrhea. When I opened his diaper, I was not prepared for what I found. His genitals were crusted and raw. His little anus was also red and raw. The baby learned that crying didn't bring him any immediate comfort, so he didn't cry. The baby used to pull his hair from the back of his head when he was in distress. He had little bold spots at the bottom of his skull. It was so painful for me to see this.

Agustin saw my face of shock when I opened his diaper. But I knew how to handle the situation. I immediately informed Agustin that I wanted the Pediatrician who took care of William to come to our room tomorrow morning, no matter the cost. He said he would arrange it immediately. After he left, Edwin asked me if I was going to follow the feeding schedule. I told him absolutely not.

That evening, I didn't know how to bathe William. I didn't want to hurt him. I placed him in very luke-warm water and tried not to touch him. He didn't cry at all. I cried for him. I had bought Desitin for diaper rash, so I just placed it all over his little private parts and his little anus for comfort.

He had a pacifier that was his life. He slept holding the pacifier with two hands over his mouth. All I could do was cry for him.

We took turns holding him and giving him as much comfort as possible. I did give him formula, but he threw up most of it. He was still very sick.

The pediatrician arrived at 9:30 a.m. the next morning. He knew William. He explained that there were many orphans and only so many hands available to take care of them. But now that he was with his mommy, he will thrive well with our love and care. He gave me a prescription for a special ointment for his genitals and anus and he gave him antibiotics as an injection. William practically had no muscle in his little butt for such a huge injection. But he didn't cry at all. That's okay, I cried for him.

I told him that he threw up the formula and he instructed that I dilute it, so he could tolerate it better. He gave me the ratio to follow. I used whatever bottle I was given to feed him. I learned with Marisa not to change that until I got to the States.

I bought a little wind-up toy with me that played peek-a-boo and he loved the little toy. Every day we went out for a walk at 10:30 a.m. with William. We walked him around the perimeter of the hotel, and we learned the location of the pharmacy, marketplace, and little restaurants to eat that were in proximity to the hotel.

We also learned that Paraguay was having Democratic elections for the first time. So, every time there was going to be a political campaign by the candidates, the US Consulate would let us know not to venture out near these locations, or simply stay in the hotel. We did as we were instructed. We met some of the other couples who were adopting, and we got close to a couple adopting a little girl who was about eighteen months. She was so cute. We often hung out together, whenever it was possible.

One day we had an appointment and couldn't take William for a walk. Suddenly, when 10:30 a.m. passed, William started to cry! "Oh my God," I said. "William wants something!" It was the first time he cried. I looked at Edwin and remarked, "He wants his walk." So, I said, "Let's go, even if we just pace back and forth in front of the Hotel waiting for Agustin, he will get his little walk." As soon as we left, he stopped crying. I was crying too, out of happiness.

After one week, we started to see improvement in William's demeanor and skin color. He was smiling at us and started to hold his head up, cooing every time I would wind up his little peek-a-boo toy. He loved that toy.

In the second week with us, William started to cry more and learned quickly that we would provide love and comfort and nourishment. He started to thrive. I was so happy that he was starting to bond with us! It's amazing to witness firsthand how love works miracles.

We were set to leave Paraguay in three weeks-time. It was kismet because, we arrived once again in New York on Mother's Day. It was so unreal because we arrived on Mother's Day five years ago with Marisa! But, it wasn't without drama. The elections were set to take place on the very day that we were leaving Asuncion and I was worried that roads would be blocked, and we couldn't get to the airport in time for our flight. We decided to leave extra early, but not without all this political drama unfolding in Asuncion.

Our plane had a layover in Sao Paulo, but we were leaving on the same plane to New York. I didn't know that we had to deplane, get our luggage, and get re-ticketed for the flight to New York. I had just fed William on the plane. The stewardess approached us and let us know that we indeed had to deplane because it was an international flight. Well, with all the movement, William ended up throwing up all his formula. Consequently, Edwin had vomit all down his shirt. What could we do? Edwin simply washed up in the men's room as best he could.

At the time, smoking was allowed in the waiting areas and ventilation was awful where we were seated with an infant. I couldn't wait to get on the plane and get away from all that smoke. There was no space that was smoke free. So many people were smoking cigarettes and some men were smoking cigars. It was simply awful and affected William's little lungs tremendously. Within in a few days of being home, William developed respiratory distress and we rushed him to the hospital. He had to be admitted. When the physicians let me see him, I saw William exhibiting behavior similar to when we first got him. He had both his little hands on top of his pacifier. The doctors had him in an oxygen tent and I couldn't touch him. I tried to reach him with my voice, but this had no reaction. I thought hard on what behavior I could do that would let him know that *I didn't abandon him.* I remembered the wind-up toy he loved. So, I told my husband to rush home and get that toy! I was so devastated watching him. As soon as I got the toy, I wound it up. When the toy played its little song, William's little face turned toward the toy and, in that instant, his whole demeanor changed. In truth, I saw firsthand that only <u>love</u> is real. He instantly knew that I was still there with him. I started to cry from pure joy. William stayed in the hospital for one whole week. After the fourth day, I could hold him and feed him. He was so happy to feel my warmth. I was so very grateful. As a direct consequence, William had to have asthma treatments for the first three years of his little life. We managed.

On the day I arrived with William at JFK, Mom, Dad, and Marisa were waiting for us. Our flight arrived quite early in the morning. I was so happy to see them all. Mom immediately took William from me and she couldn't believe how adorable he was. She smothered him with kisses. Marisa was a bit standoffish when she saw us. Maybe she was a bit angry that we left her. I didn't get the reaction that I thought I was going to get... a big hug and kiss. I was disappointed, but I let it be. She was entitled to her feelings. Maybe she was scared we would leave her again. It had to be difficult for her. I remember sometimes, Marisa didn't want to talk to us on the phone. It was too hard for her.

When I arrived at home, mom had decorated our house with Welcome Home signs for the baby and had Happy Mother's Day gifts for me and the baby. Slowly, family was starting to filter into our home. Marisa became excited and happy to finally be in her home again with mommy and daddy, and now, a new baby brother. She started to come around. I was giving her space, but I felt relieved when I saw her happy and excited.

I was so very tired. William was so happy, taking everything in. He was cooing, smiling, and laughing. Everyone was so in awe of him. Taking turns to hold him, kiss him and he was clearly loving all the attention. He deserved all that love and more after being in an orphanage for four months. My son, William, is home! We are once again grateful for all our blessings, and support from our parents and loving family.

Here are some pics:

First Day with William

He was so scared!

William Coming Home with Marisa

The Two Williams

Me with My Loving Babies

William and Marisa

ONLY LOVE IS REAL!

If you are interested in finding out about international adoptions, visit the LAPA-Latin American Parents Association web site:

http://www.lapa.com

or https://lapa-ncr.clubexpress.com.

Clari Diaz

ABOUT THE AUTHOR

Clari is an adoptive parent. Her children are now adults and she has their approval to publish this book. She travels between two homes, one in Westchester County, the other in Puerto Rico. She loves the diversity of both places. Clari is now retired. In her professional career, she worked as a Physician Leadership Recruiter for Memorial Sloan Kettering Cancer Center. She had a career in healthcare administration that spanned close to thirty years. She especially loved her work as a recruiter, as she had the honor of meeting the most incredible and talented physician scientist leaders from all over the world. She also helped physicians in their professional career growth and met many young, upcoming physicians through her membership in the Association of Hispanic Healthcare Executives. One of her close colleagues remarked that she could read a CV like tea leaves.

She now enjoys being a grandmother and cooking. She has a Facebook group called "Cooking with Clari," which focuses on Puerto Rican cookery and its traditions. She is currently working on her second cookbook. She wrote, "Cooking and Telling Stories y El Pilon."

She hopes this new book brings insight and hope to people interested in adopting a child.